Daniel Study Guide

Daniel
STUDY GUIDE

Michael Lewis

The Christadelphian
404 Shaftmoor Lane, Hall Green, Birmingham B28 8SZ, UK
©2008 The Christadelphian Magazine & Publishing Association Limited

First published 2008
ISBN 978 0 85189 184 2

Cover photograph:
Lion relief from the Processional Way leading to the Ishtar Gate in Babylon
(Pergamon Museum, Berlin)

Printed in England by:

The Cromwell Press
TROWBRIDGE BA14 0XB

Contents

What is a Study Guide?

1 **Aims:** The overriding aim of all Bible study is that through knowledge and understanding of the word of God a person may become "wise unto salvation through faith which is in Christ Jesus" (2 Timothy 3:15).

"Study Guides" are designed to explain the straightforward teachings of scripture and where appropriate to emphasise:

a)   First principles of doctrine

b)   Practical outcomes

They should be helpful to young people, to those who are "young in the faith", who often have very little background knowledge of the scriptures, and to those of all ages and experience who enjoy straightforward, uncomplicated study of the Bible.

2 **Other features of Study Guides**

a) **Layout:** After a brief introduction to the book, essential background information is provided before looking at the text in more detail. Headings and verse references make it easy to use the guide for looking up information on any section of the Bible text.

b) **Bible versions:** This Guide mainly uses the New King James Version as a basis, as this helps to overcome problems of archaic expressions that exist in the Authorised (King James) Version (AV / KJV), which remains the most used translation in Christadelphian ecclesias today. Other versions can sometimes assist in clarifying a particular passage, but some popular modern versions are unreliable and betray the doctrinal bias of their translators.

c) **Manageable sections:** Each Guide is divided into units of study which are not too long. This will make it easier for individuals or groups to make progress. An hour's concentrated and productive study on a regular basis is likely to yield good results.

d) **Visual help:** The prophets and the Lord Jesus himself used visual illustrations to communicate their message. While the prime emphasis is on the written word, visual help is given wherever possible to increase understanding.

e) **Use alongside the Bible:** The student must have a Bible open alongside the Guide.

It is recommended at the outset that important information is marked in the Bible. Have a pencil at the ready.

f) **Further study:** The final sections contain suggestions for further study and a book list chosen on the basis of sound expositional and doctrinal content.

g) **Prayer:** We are studying the word of God. Before commencing any Bible study we must ask God's blessing on our activity. Thank God for making the Bible available to us, so that through it we may come to know Him and to look forward to His coming kingdom.

Here is a prayer that sums up our aim:

"Open thou mine eyes, that I may behold wondrous things out of thy law."
(Psalm 119:18)

Preface

THE book of Daniel is an endless source of fascination to its readers. In its pages we find thrilling visions of the kingdom of God, the first clear statement about the sacrifice of the Lord Jesus, dramatic trials of faith for God's people and details of life at the courts of Babylon and Persia. All this in twelve relatively short chapters.

It is also a challenge because much of it is not easy to understand. The purpose of this Study Guide is to make a start in opening up the book for those who would like to know what Daniel is telling us but don't know where to begin. It is not a verse by verse commentary but an attempt to see what the book has to say to 21st century believers. The last section points the way to more detailed study for those who are as excited by the message of Daniel as I am. The Guide can be used for straightforward personal reading or as a basis for group study.

Anyone writing about Bible prophecy is faced with an immediate problem. What about those prophecies yet to be fulfilled? Should we speculate on the outcome? There is a wise rule among Bible students that we should not, but rather wait until the events have occurred when we can see the fulfilment beyond doubt. It is a guideline that has underpinned the review of Daniel's prophecies in this Study Guide. There are two or three exceptions to this, where speculation was felt necessary in order to communicate the prophecy's meaning fully, or to convey some information which may be relevant to its fulfilment. But the speculation has been limited and should be recognised as coming into this category.

Like all of the Bible, the book of Daniel is written to glorify God and prepare men and women for His kingdom. Any time we can spend with Daniel's inspired words will help each of us to draw nearer to the Father. The aim of this Study Guide is to do just that and bring each of us a little closer to understanding the words of this remarkable servant of God.

MICHAEL LEWIS

Acknowledgments

The publishers express their gratitude for the following illustrations:

- The illustration of Nebuchadnezzar's image (pages 10, 16), the beasts in Daniel 7 (pages 10, 34), and the illustrations on pages 19, 23, 25, 31, 57, 61, 62 – Paul Wasson.
- Tinting of illustrations on pages 19, 23, 25, 31, 57, all maps, and other illustrations – Mark Norris.

Introduction

THE book of Daniel is important reading for followers of the Lord Jesus. Both the Lord and the Apostle Paul directed believers to its pages for guidance and support. We want to find out why this is so and discover what the book has to say to disciples today.

A quick reading shows that it is a series of visions from the Lord God about future events on the world stage. These visions are given either directly to Daniel or through dreams. It is one of the 'Apocalyptic' books, a term used for prophecies such as Revelation which foretell what is going to happen on the earth. Apocalypse in the Bible means literally an 'uncovering' or a 'revealing' of events still in the future. The message is given through visions, often built around symbols such as the image of a man or animals. Daniel and Revelation are distinguished by having a series of these visions, each of which take us from a point in history to the kingdom of God.

But like all prophecy, the purpose of Daniel's writings is to *"make ready a people prepared for the Lord"* (Luke 1:17). It was never God's intention to make His people political commentators. Prophecy is designed to help them grow in their faith.

Although the book of Daniel is best known for its visions, a significant amount of it is devotional, that is about people serving God in the way that is pleasing to Him.

The events behind the book

As the world approached 600 BC the power of mighty Assyria was waning. Babylon was the rising star, with Nebuchadnezzar its remarkable military leader lining up his nation to take over as the world super-power. But it would not be easy. Pharaoh-Neco brought his Egyptian armies to the defence of Assyria and swept up the Mediterranean coast. Josiah, king of Judah, made an ill-fated attempt to stop him (2 Kings 23:28-30), and Judah came under the control of Egypt. In 605 BC Nebuchadnezzar defeated Pharaoh at the battle of Carchemish and took over all Egypt's territories including Judah. So began the seventy year domination of the Jews by Babylon, long foretold by the prophets and which provides the backdrop to the book of Daniel.

Nebuchadnezzar came against Jerusalem three times, in 605, 597 and 587 BC, each time with increasing severity. Following the customs of his day, he took back to Babylon anyone in Judah who he thought might be useful to him. Daniel and his friends were among those carried away in 605 BC.

Who wrote the book?

Daniel was quite young when he left Judah, probably in his late teens. He was among the nobility of the nation, possibly a member of the royal family. He would have been greatly influenced as a boy by the reforms of King Josiah. He would also have been affected by the words of the prophet Jeremiah. He is one of three righteous men listed in Ezekiel 14:14. Within his own book he is described three times as a man *"greatly beloved"*. Daniel appears to have lived the rest of his life in exile and there is no record of his returning to Israel, even after Cyrus' decree in 538 BC. Possibly Daniel was too old by then to make the arduous journey.

We know Daniel was a prophet and wrote the book named after him because the Lord Jesus tells us so (Matthew 24:15). In the first six chapters Daniel writes in the third person, that is he writes about the events in which he played a key role and interpreting the dreams. In the last six chapters he writes in the first person, directly recording the visions and surrounding events to see the difference (compare 1:17-21 and 10:2-9). Some have claimed that Daniel did not write the first half of the book, but there is a unity about all twelve chapters which leads to the conclusion there is only one author.

The two languages

Although it is part of the Old Testament which is written in Hebrew, a large section of the book (2:4 to 7:28) is written in Aramaic.

Aramaic is similar to Hebrew and shares the same script. It was an international language (2 Kings 18:26), common in

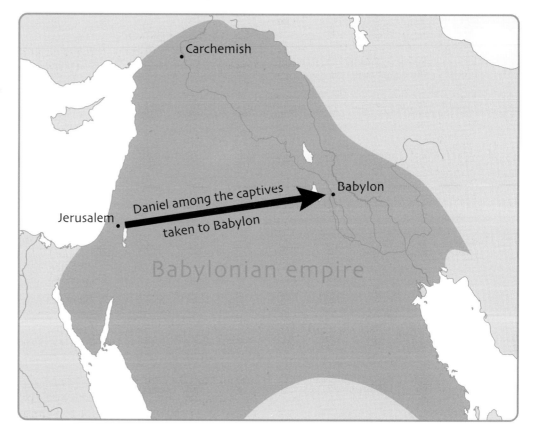

A word about dates

There are two things to bear in mind:

1 Dates for key events vary slightly from one history book to another. This is simply because nobody really knows. But they only vary by a year or two and do not affect the message of the book which is our concern.

2 When the Bible quotes the year of a king's reign there may be a difference between two passages. An example is the beginning of Nebuchadnezzar's rule over Judah which Jeremiah states was the fourth year of Jehoiakim (25:1) but Daniel calls the third year of Jehoiakim (1:1). This is because Nebuchadnezzar came to power in September 605. Jeremiah was using the Hebrew method which counts the year in which the king ascended to the throne as the first year (i.e. 605), but Daniel is using the Babylonian method which only recognises full years so it will always be the year following accession which is the first year of the reign (i.e. 604).

Babylon and Persia. We cannot be certain why it is used in Daniel but the sections where it is used centre on Gentiles, notably Nebuchadnezzar, Darius and their royal courts. Both kings were greatly influenced by Daniel and his friends to the extent that they fully recognised the God of Israel and it is possible that the section in Aramaic was issued on its own as a kind of preaching booklet.

When was it written?

As Daniel was the author the events and prophecies must have been written down during the exile (605-536 BC). However, the prophecies in Chapter 11 are so detailed and their fulfilment has been so accurate that Bible critics have claimed the book must have been written after the events, in the second century BC. Arguments in favour of the view that the book was written in Daniel's time include:

- internal evidence showing Daniel knew all about life at court in Babylonian and Persian times. Almost certainly this would not have been known to a writer in the second century BC but has been confirmed by recent excavations.
- much of the prophecy goes beyond the second century BC but has still been fulfilled accurately. The seventy weeks prophecy of Chapter 9 is a good example.

The order of the chapters

Each chapter in the book begins with the name of the king in power at the time, usually giving the year of his reign. They are not in chronological order: chapters 5 and 6 relate to events that took place after the visions of chapters 7 and 8.

On to the message of Daniel …

Having looked at this background information we now move on to the book itself. The next section is an overview and a summary of Daniel's message. After that the sections look first at the four main prophecies as a group and then work through the book a chapter at a time. There is "Further reading" at the end for those who want answers to questions of detail not covered in this Study Guide.

What are the chapters about?

1   **The setting of the book.** Daniel and his friends are taken to Babylon where they immediately have to deal with the problem of being God's servants in an ungodly world.

2   **FIRST PROPHECY:** Daniel interprets Nebuchadnezzar's dream. It is the symbolic image of a man made of four metals that foretell key events until the kingdom of God is established.

3   **The fiery furnace.** Daniel's three friends are thrown into the fiery furnace for refusing to worship Nebuchadnezzar's image. God delivers them.

4   **Nebuchadnezzar's illness.** Through illness and a dream interpreted by Daniel, Nebuchadnezzar is taught that God is in control of world affairs and he is only a great king because it is God's will.

5   **Belshazzar's feast.** In an act of bravado Belshazzar uses the cups from the temple at Jerusalem for his own feasting. God tells him through Daniel that the end of Babylon has been decreed.

6   **Daniel in the lions' den.** Under Darius the Mede Daniel is thrown into the lions' den for continuing to worship God. God delivers him.

7   **SECOND PROPHECY:** A vision is given to Daniel of four symbolic beasts which correspond to the four metals of Nebuchadnezzar's image of chapter 2 and foretell the same key events. But this vision gives us much more detail and a different perspective.

8-9   **THIRD PROPHECY:**

–   Chapter 8. The vision follows the same path as the previous prophecies with symbolic animals taking us through key events that lead to the kingdom of God. But this time we see the impact on Israel and events at the time of the Lord Jesus including his sacrifice.

–   Chapter 9. Daniel prays for the forgiveness of his people's sins which led to the exile. The answer to his prayer is a more detailed explanation of the vision in the previous chapter. It is the seventy weeks prophecy which ends with the sacrifice of the Lord Jesus and the complete forgiveness of sins.

10-12 **FOURTH PROPHECY:**

–   Chapter 10. Daniel sees the angel sent to give the vision and is reduced to a state of great weakness. His condition becomes a symbolic death from which the angel resurrects and strengthens him to the point where he can receive the vision.

–   Chapter 11. The main part of the vision foretells future events which go through to the time of the end, some in great detail.

–   Chapter 12. The vision concludes by taking us to the second coming of the Lord Jesus and the establishment of the kingdom of God.

Overview

THE kingdom of God is at the core of Daniel's message. As the book develops, he shows us that:

- The Lord God is in control of events on earth and has set a time limit on human rulership. It will be replaced by His kingdom which will last for ever.

- Before that could happen, Messiah had to come and offer his life to enable the faithful to have eternal life in the kingdom.

- Men and women who understand and believe these truths become different people, and their lives are changed because they are focused on the kingdom of God.

1. The kingdom of God

When the Lord God looks down on the earth He sees only two kingdoms, the **kingdom of men** and the **kingdom of God**. The kingdom of men is the world under human rule. It has gone through many phases in history and covered endless national boundaries yet in the sight of God it is only one kingdom. It is human rebellion, man laying claim to ownership of the earth and wanting to rule it his way. The kingdom of men has always been in conflict with the kingdom of God but the outcome is never in doubt and the book of Daniel ends with the complete triumph of divine rule through the Lord Jesus Christ. At the heart of the message we discover that, whatever man may think, it is the Lord God who is in control and is moving steadily towards the fulfilment of His purpose with the earth. Through four great prophecies the book gives us the steps that will be taken in human history from Daniel's own time to the inevitable conclusion:

- The four prophecies tell of the end of human rulership and the setting up of God's kingdom.

- The image of Nebuchadnezzar's dream in chapter 2 includes four empires, but it is only one 'man' because in God's sight it is only one kingdom, the kingdom of men.

- A key phrase is given three times in chapter 4, *"the Most High rules in the kingdom of men"* (verses 17,25,32). God is in control of events on earth. (NB. The word 'kingdom' is singular, confirming there is only one kingdom of human rulership from God's perspective.)

- Belshazzar's feast in chapter 5 was a rebellion against God and typifies the thinking of the kingdom of men. By using cups from God's temple at Jerusalem for his drunken feasting he was making a statement that men have triumphed over the God of heaven. He didn't last long.

2. The sacrifice of the Lord Jesus

The purpose of God is to glorify Himself through His kingdom on the earth. He loves all men and women and wants us to be with Him in the kingdom. That is not possible in our present sinful state. Therefore He has provided the Lord Jesus as a sacrifice for our sins and this is foretold in the book of Daniel. Daniel puts the sacrifice of Jesus in its right perspective – in the context of the kingdom of God. First come the prophecies of the kingdom, then we learn about the sacrifice of Christ. When the kingdom is established the sacrifice of the Lord Jesus will enable men and women to enter it and become part of the glory of God. Salvation is not just for our benefit, it is an expression of God's glory.

The chapters that tell us about the sacrifice of the Lord Jesus are:

- Chapter 8 – the last empire, Rome, will *"rise against the Prince of princes"* (verse 25), foretelling the crucifixion of Jesus by the Romans.
- Chapter 9 – The seventy weeks prophecy gives a sequence of events leading up to the sacrifice of Christ.

3. The impact on men and women

Disciples are committed to the worship of God and want to be in the kingdom. They are seeking to live according to God's commands. Because they are living in the kingdom of men, which is ruled by human values, they live different lives from those around them. From time to time that difference may result in persecution. What Daniel makes clear is that God's will comes first:

- Daniel and his friends refuse to eat the food offered to them at the Babylonian court because it was contrary to God's will (chapter 1).
- The three friends are thrown into the fiery furnace because they will not bow down and worship the golden image (chapter 3).
- Daniel himself is thrown into the lions' den because he will not hold back from worshipping God (chapter 6).
- God's people are persecuted as a result of their obedience to God's law (chapter 11).

The Bible in miniature

These three great themes are not only the teaching of Daniel, they are the central message of scripture. In this sense the book of Daniel can be viewed as the Bible in miniature, a simple view of God's plan and purpose with the earth. It would not be complete without the constant reminder of God's support for those who seek Him as they wrestle with sin in all its forms.

The four prophecies

FOUR great prophecies form the backbone of the book of Daniel and the rest of the message is woven around them. They are illustrated in the chart on page 10. You can see straightaway that despite containing different descriptions they cover basically the same ground:

- Four empires will play a dominant role from the time of Daniel until the kingdom of God is established. The empires are Babylon, Medo-Persia, Greece and Rome.

- Human rulership will be brought to an end by the return of Jesus Christ to the earth, and the setting up of the kingdom of God.

All the prophecies have this in common but then we find that each has something different to tell us as well. In this section we shall look briefly at the elements that are the same and also suggest what we can learn from the differences. Although the prophecies cover events on the world stage they are nevertheless selective. There is no attempt to capture the whole of world history. Only those events which affect God's people are prophesied, firstly Israel and secondly all the faithful, both Jew and Gentile.

Nebuchadnezzar's dream image (chapter 2)

Nebuchadnezzar's dream was an image of a man. The parts of the body were made from different metals and each represented one of the empires to come. The important point is that the image was of only one man even though it included all four empires. The kingdom of men may have different phases through history but is still one kingdom in God's sight. To men the image appeared most impressive, an image *"whose splendour was excellent ... and its form was awesome"* (verse 31). This is how people see the world around us, but this mighty image is brought to an end by a little stone striking it on the feet. It is replaced by the kingdom of God. The stone was *"cut out without hands"*, meaning it was to be God's work not man's and we know it refers to the Lord Jesus Christ and his second coming (Daniel 2:45; Matthew 21:42-44; 1 Corinthians 15:23-28).

The four beasts (chapter 7)

Daniel's vision was of four different beasts, three of them corresponding to known animals. Each beast stands for one of the four empires revealed by the image of chapter 2, but there are differences that are instructive. In chapter 2 was an awesome image of a man which is how people see the world. In chapter 7 we see the same empires through God's eyes. He likens them to beasts because men are only following natural instincts and not rising above them to follow His will. We also get much more detail. All human government will be taken away by the death of the fourth beast and the earth will be given to the Lord Jesus and His people.

The evening-morning vision (chapters 8-9)

By the time Daniel received this vision the end of the Babylonian empire was near so it was not included in the prophecy. We find only the last three empires, Medo-Persia, Greece and Rome. Again they are represented by animals but in a slightly different way. A ram stands for Medo-Persia. Greece and Rome are both represented by the same animal, a male goat. Greece is symbolised by one set of the goat's horns while a separate little horn is used to signify Rome.

What is different about this vision? It is at this point, the beginning of chapter 8, where the original language turns back to Hebrew, and the prophecy therefore focuses on the impact of the empires on Israel. In particular it gives details of the sacrifice of the Lord Jesus and the destruction of Jerusalem in AD 70. In common with the other prophecies, it takes us to the time of the end when the fourth empire is *"broken without human means"*,

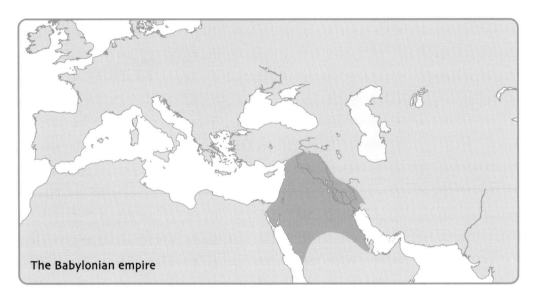

The Babylonian empire

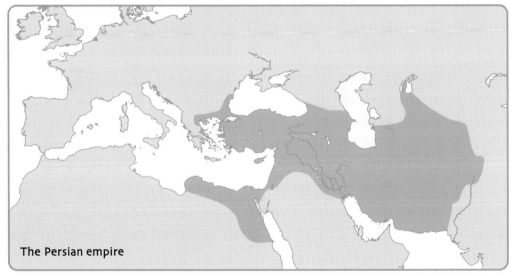

The Persian empire

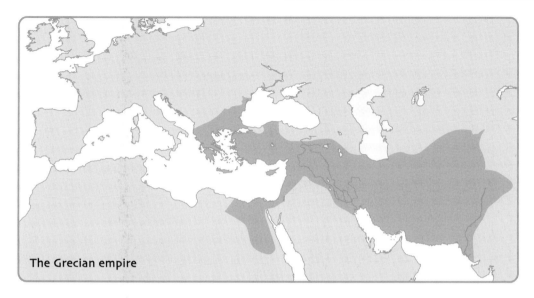

The Grecian empire

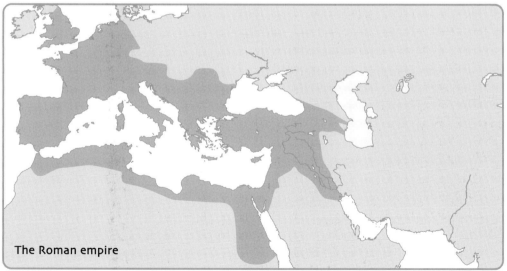

The Roman empire

a direct parallel to the *"stone cut out without hands"* in chapter 2.

The final vision (chapters 10-12)

By the time the fourth prophecy was given to Daniel, Babylon had been overrun by Medo-Persia, so again only the last three empires appear. Symbols are not used: the entire message is spoken by the angel. The prophecy follows the same pattern as the previous visions. The key difference is that we get very detailed prophecies about particular periods of history, including the last days before the kingdom of God is established. One of these periods was a time of severe persecution for faithful Jewish people. This detailed account of events in advance provides support for God's people when it is really needed. They can see that God is still in control. The prophecy takes us to the time of the end. People under persecution can see that the kingdom of men will eventually be taken away and the kingdom of God established.

Summary

It is important to see how these prophecies fit together because they bring home the overall message of Daniel. All history is moving towards the setting up of God's kingdom. Each of the prophecies has this in common. When we look at them more closely we find that the differences between the prophecies provide encouragement for God's people in their different circumstances.

Date	Empire	Chapter 2	Chapter 7	Chapter 8	Chapter 11
605 BC	Babylon	Head of gold	The lion		
538 BC	Medo-Persia	Chest and arms of silver	The bear	The ram	verse 2
331 BC	Greece	Belly and thighs of bronze	The leopard	The male goat (great horn and four horns)	verses 3-35
63 BC	Rome	Legs of iron	The terrible beast	The male goat (little horn)	verses 36-39
circa AD 1800		Feet of iron and clay			
The kingdom		Stone cut without hands	The beast was slain	Broken without human means	He shall come to his end

Into exile

DANIEL CHAPTER 1

DRAMATIC events show the impact on God's servants of living in an ungodly environment. Daniel and his three friends are taken from Judah to live in Babylon and to work at the court of Nebuchadnezzar. Because Babylon has a completely different religion and set of values they are immediately faced with difficulties. They make a stand for their faith even though it could cost them their lives, and they are delivered. Under God's guidance, they rise to become the foremost among the advisers of Nebuchadnezzar.

WHEN Nebuchadnezzar plundered the temple in Jerusalem and took its treasures back to Babylon in 605 BC he was claiming that his gods must be greater than the God of Israel. Outwardly this appeared to be the case but Daniel's insight gives a different perspective. Speaking of Nebuchadnezzar he says, *"the Lord gave Jehoiakim king of Judah into his hand"* (1:2). This establishes the main theme of the book at the outset, that the Lord God is in control of events and He gave Judah into Babylon's power.

As well as implements from the temple a small group of people were also taken. They were to be on Nebuchadnezzar's staff and so had to be good-looking, bright and young. Daniel and his friends were probably teenagers when they made the journey from their homeland to Babylon. What awaited them there was a three-year course of studies with Chaldean tutors, considered essential before they could start to work for the king (verses 3-5).

Problems

Most young people of the day would have rejoiced at the opportunities for personal advancement this created, but Daniel and his friends were not interested in personal ambition. They were faithful servants of the God of Israel. Their only interest was in serving Him and the new situation presented three immediate problems:

- They were given Babylonian names which had overtones of the Babylonian religion (verse 7).
- The courses they had to undertake were only partly academic. Some of them were in the religion of the Chaldeans (verse 4).

- The food and wine they were given was contrary to the Law of Moses (verses 5,8).

There is no record about how they handled the first two, but from the stand they made on the third it is clear they had no mind to compromise. There are two possible reasons why the food and wine were unacceptable to them. They might have been used in a Babylonian religious rite of which they wanted no part. Or possibly the meat was not prepared in accordance with the law. Whatever the reason, they would not eat the food that was offered. The situation was made worse when the chief of the eunuchs, who was responsible for their welfare, confided in them that his own life was in danger as a result of their refusal to eat (verse 10). Surely a good reason to compromise! But service to God is governed by faith and commitment, not human reasoning and compromise. In a telling phrase, *"Daniel purposed in his heart"* that he would not eat of *"the king's delicacies"* (verse 8). The four highlighted words capture what is required for God's people to live a godly life in an ungodly world. The faith and commitment of Daniel and his friends were rewarded and they were always found to be well nourished.

An interview with Nebuchadnezzar

Most students have examinations at the end of their studies. Poor Daniel and his friends had to face an interview with Nebuchadnezzar! They need not have worried. Nebuchadnezzar was impressed with his four Jewish captives (verses 17-20). We are also told that *"Daniel had understanding in all visions and dreams"* (verse 17). Superficially we might think this means that Daniel had some mystic talent. Of course it was nothing of the kind. It is God's definition of a prophet (Numbers 12:6), a role that Daniel clearly filled. Combined with the phrase, *"God gave them knowledge and skill"*, it confirms that although they were in very trying circumstances Daniel and his friends were there for a purpose. As we move on to the next chapter, the first of the four great prophecies, we begin to see just what this purpose was and why the Lord God had brought them to Babylon to live at the court of king Nebuchadnezzar.

Nebuchadnezzar's image dream

DANIEL CHAPTER 2

> Nebuchadnezzar has a dream from God which can only be interpreted by Daniel and his friends. He sees the image of a man representing four great empires which must play their part in world history before they are replaced by the kingdom of God. The image stands for the kingdom of men and appears to be powerful, but in reality is quite vulnerable. It is easily brought down by a stone which grows to fill the earth.

BECAUSE of his important place in the Bible it is tempting to look favourably at Nebuchadnezzar. In fact he was a military dictator and may well have been suffering from paranoia. We are told in 2:1 that *"his spirit was so troubled that his sleep left him"*, and later Daniel provides the reason (verse 29). Nebuchadnezzar was lying awake worrying about what would happen after his reign. Would there be a greater king of Babylon? Would he be usurped as the greatest leader in history? Eventually he fell into a troubled sleep and the answers were given in a dream, although they were not the answers he expected.

It is not clear whether the king could remember the details when he woke in the morning. Even if he remembered the dream he could not understand it and his rising frustration gave way to an intense anger which expressed itself in dire threats against his servants (verses 5,12,13).

A problem for the wise men

Nebuchadnezzar assembled all the wise men who could possibly help (verses 2,3). It was an age in which people believed in the importance of dreams. The problem in this case was that Nebuchadnezzar had not told them the dream. He challenged the wise men to divine its contents for themselves, and this became the benchmark against which he would judge the correctness of their interpretation (verse 9). It was an impossible task, and the wise men were forced to acknowledge this to the king. All they could do was play for time, *"hoping the situation will change"* (verse 9, NIV).

Daniel seeks God's help (verses 14-23)

In those days Daniel and his friends were junior members of the group of 'wise men' and it was their senior colleagues who had been called to the king. Nevertheless they came under the edict of execution. Being in the Lord's service does not mean things will always go smoothly, neither is it always clear why difficulties arise. They must be accepted in humility and faith and seen as part of the chastening experiences which come to all God's children. They are essential to the development of a Christlike character as Daniel demonstrates. His response when he hears about the death sentence is an object lesson in how God's people should react to such situations:

- He spoke to Arioch, the captain of the king's guard with *"wisdom and tact"* (verse 14, NIV). There was no question of his arguing, being difficult or insisting on his rights. That is man's way, not God's. The Apostle Paul teaches, *"… a servant of the Lord must not quarrel but be gentle to all, able to teach, patient, in humility correcting those who are in opposition"* (2 Timothy 2:24,25).

- He discussed the problem with his friends (verse 17). No one has all the answers, including Daniel.

- Above all he sought God's guidance (verse 18). *"If any of you lacks wisdom, let him ask of God, who gives to all liberally and without reproach, and it will be given to him"* (James 1:5).

So the dream and its interpretation were given to Daniel in a night vision (verse 19). Sometimes this chapter is called "Nebuchadnezzar's dream", but the real message came in a vision to Daniel.

Daniel's response is like a psalm, full of heartfelt praise and thanksgiving (verses 20-23). It states clearly for the first time in the book that God is in control of events and will reveal what is going on to those who are wise. To these God will reveal *"deep and secret things"* because He *"knows what is in the darkness, and light dwells with Him"*. The world is a place of darkness and God's light is needed to reveal what is happening and where the world is heading. He revealed to Daniel what the king wanted to know.

The dream and its interpretation (verses 24-45)

So Daniel made his way to Nebuchadnezzar. He first of all attributed his success completely to God, taking no credit for himself (verses 27-30).

The dream was initially a response to Nebuchadnezzar's anxiety about the future. In it he was watching, observing events to see what would happen. He saw the image of a man with each of the main parts of the body represented by a metal. The head was of fine gold, the chest and arms of silver, the belly and thighs of bronze, the legs of iron, the feet a mixture of iron and clay. In his dream, Nebuchadnezzar observed this statue and then watched while a stone prepared without human skill struck the image on the feet and broke them. Inevitably the statue could not stay upright and it toppled to the ground. The stone grew. It crushed the metals into pieces so small and light they were blown

Who were the Chaldeans?

In most translations of the Bible the Chaldeans appear in the book of Daniel in two ways:

➤ As a race, originally a Semitic tribe that migrated from Syria to the Persian Gulf. They mingled with the Babylonian people but rapidly became the more powerful group producing most of the kings and rulers including Nebuchadnezzar (5:30, 9:1).

➤ As practitioners of the astrology for which they were famous (2:2,4,5). They were a kind of priesthood and their discipline probably included various forms of divination, hence the request of Nebuchadnezzar for help with his dream.

away by the wind to disappear for ever. But the stone continued to grow until it was a mountain that filled the earth.

Each of the metals represented a kingdom or empire. The head of fine gold was Babylon, Nebuchadnezzar's kingdom. It ruled the known world of the day and all people, animals and birds came under its control. But in answer to Nebuchadnezzar's unspoken question the image revealed that Babylon would not last for ever. It would be succeeded by another empire represented by the chest and arms of silver. As silver is of lesser quality than gold, so this second kingdom would be inferior to Babylon. In turn it would give way to another empire, the belly and thighs of bronze, but still one that ruled the world. The most inferior metal, iron, is used to depict the fourth empire, the legs of the image. This kingdom was to be different from the others, having immense strength that it would use to shatter and crush all opposition. The iron continued into the feet, but now with clay alongside it because the kingdom would be divided. It would still contain the strength of the legs of iron but now include the weakness of clay. Finally, at the time of the end the fourth empire would have ten separate powers within it, represented by the toes of the image. We get more detail about these powers when we come to chapter 7. It is in the time of the toes that God would intervene and establish His own kingdom on the earth.

The prophecy leaves its readers to work out the identity of the human empires after

Babylon. But the final part is set out with unquestioned clarity. At the end of the time represented by the four metals and the clay God Himself will set up a kingdom which will last for ever. It will take over the earth and put an end to human rule. Above all it will *"not be left to other people"*; that is, it will have no successor like each of the human empires, instead *"it shall stand forever"*.

What is the meaning of the vision?

Nebuchadnezzar was overjoyed because his fears were unfounded. The succeeding empires would all be inferior to his and it appeared he would be the greatest king in history. But the dream was not given to satisfy Nebuchadnezzar. It was, and is, a message to all who want to know the truth about why we are here and where the world is heading. It is a message of light for a dark world. It shows that God will not always allow things to continue as they are but will intervene to bring man's rule to an end. And by setting out the milestones of human history that will arise before this great event occurs, the vision provides a steady flow of evidence that it is true and the kingdom of God will come. God's people can be encouraged and strengthened, particularly in difficult times by this ongoing confirmation that the divine purpose is heading towards its magnificent completion.

It is not difficult to see the fulfilment of the prophecy. A glance at world history shows that everything Daniel said came true. The Medo-Persian empire took over from Babylon. It was followed by the Greek empire which was in turn succeeded by the Roman. The Roman empire split into two parts, east and west, represented by the two legs of the image. The table shows how these empires relate to the metals and their dates. One thing to be noted is that the Roman empire ended in approximately AD 500, yet the iron of the image lasts until the kingdom of God which is still future. The prophecy therefore requires there to be a significant power that has existed in Rome from the time of the end of the empire to the present day and looks set to carry on in the future. It is not difficult to see the fulfilment of this either. The Catholic Church, as the leader of a corrupt form of Christianity, emerged during the later years of the Roman empire and has evolved to fill the role it has today. We shall see that this identification of corrupt Christianity as the fulfilment of the iron in modern times is confirmed by subsequent visions in the book. The power of this prophecy should not be underestimated. Daniel gave the interpretation in approximately 600 BC. He had probably never heard of Rome. To identify it as an empire that would not only take over the known world but remain a significant world player for 2,500 years is not humanly possible. It puts the divine stamp on Daniel's words from the outset.

Is there any significance in the metals that are used? We are not given any by Daniel, though we can possibly note how

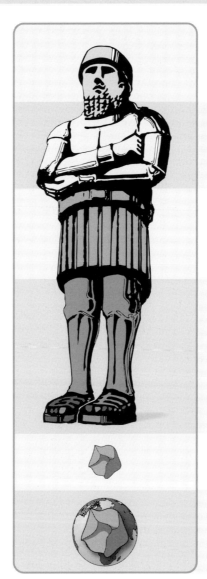

The dream	Its fulfilment
Head of fine gold	Babylon 605-538 BC
Chest and arms of silver	Medo-Persia 538-331 BC
Belly and thighs of bronze	Greece 331-63 BC
Legs of iron / Feet partly of iron and partly of clay	Rome and its successors / 63 BC to the kingdom
The stone cut out without hands	The return of the Lord Jesus
A great mountain filling the earth	The kingdom of God

decreasing value contrasts with an increasing strength.

Lessons to be learnt

In seeking to understand the message of Daniel there are a number of points in this vision that stand out:

- Although the prophecy reveals history in advance from the time of Babylon onwards, the focus is on the kingdom of God. When Daniel began his interpretation he told the king it was about *"what will be in the latter days"* (verse 28).

- The vision makes clear that God is in control. *"The God of heaven has given you a kingdom, power, strength, and glory; and wherever the children of men dwell, or the beasts of the field and the birds of the heaven, He has given them into your hand, and has made you ruler over them all"* (verses 37,38).

- The image is of four empires but one man, the kingdom of men. The image was large and dazzling – but it was vulnerable. The head was gold, the heaviest metal, so it was top heavy and would topple easily when struck on the feet. In scripture the head represents a way of thinking, in this case human thinking, and this is instrumental in the downfall of the kingdom of men.

- The image or kingdom of men will be *"crushed together"* (verse 35), that is,

the modern successors of the various empires portrayed by the image will be present at the time of the end, and will be destroyed all together.

Nebuchadnezzar's response (verses 46-49)

The king was greatly impressed with what Daniel had told him (verses 46-49). In a burst of enthusiasm he promoted Daniel to one of the key posts in the empire, the governor of Babylon itself. Daniel in turn ensured that the king knew of the part played by his three friends in the dramatic events.

Nebuchadnezzar also gave praise to the God of Israel. This may not mean as much as it seems; he was probably just adding another god to his list. Quite how much of the vision he really understood at this stage is not clear. The events of the next chapter suggest he still had a way to go in grasping the overall message of Daniel.

The new names

The young Jewish exiles were given new Babylonian names:

➤ Daniel *(God is my judge)* became Belteshazzar *(Belet defend the king)*. Bel was another name for Marduk, the patron god of Babylon and Belet was his wife.

➤ Hananiah *(God is gracious)* became Shadrak *(I am very fearful [of a god])*.

➤ Mishael *(Who is as God?)* became Meshach *(I am of very little account)*.

➤ Azariah *(God is a helper)* became Abed Nego *(Servant of the shining one)*, possibly a word play on the name of the god *Nebo*.

The important message behind these changes is that the world quickly puts pressure on us to change our identity to conform to the worship of its gods.

The land of Shinar

Although the captives were taken to Babylon, we are told that they were *"carried into the land of Shinar"* (verse 2). This is the ancient name for the part of the world in which Babylon was situated. But why use it here? It is recorded in Genesis 10:8-12 that Nimrod founded his kingdom in Shinar. He typified the man of the world (the phrase *"before the Lord"* in Genesis 10 simply means the Lord observed, not that He approved of what Nimrod was doing). In Genesis 11 the Tower of Babel is built in Shinar, a building which symbolised man's rebellion against God, his desire to wrest ownership of the earth away from God and rule it in his own way. Daniel and his friends were taken to the place where the foundations of the kingdom of men were laid, setting the scene for the conflict between the kingdom of men and the kingdom of God which is the theme of his book.

The iron and the clay

DANIEL CHAPTER 2

LOOKING at the vision of chapter 2 it is clear that almost all of it has been fulfilled except the last phase before the kingdom is established, represented by the feet of iron and clay. The purpose of this section is to look more closely at this final phase of the vision. One point to note – prophecy is best interpreted in hindsight and we are still living in the time when the iron and clay phase is being fulfilled. It is not advisable to be dogmatic in these circumstances so the interpretation offered here is only a suggestion.

The prophecy of iron and clay and its meaning

Daniel gives the meaning and significance of the feet and toes of the image being partly of iron and partly of clay:

- *"The kingdom shall be divided"* (verse 41).
- *"The strength of the iron shall be in it"* (verse 41).
- *"The kingdom shall be partly strong and partly fragile"* (verse 42).
- *"As you saw iron mixed with ceramic clay, they will mingle with the seed of men"* (verse 43).

- *"But they will not adhere to one another, just as iron does not mix with clay"* (verse 43).

How is the prophecy to be understood? The iron must be a continuation of the iron of the legs, the fourth empire, otherwise a different symbol would be used. This is confirmed by the iron retaining the strength it had before (verses 40,41) and this feature will continue until the time of the end. The iron of the feet is therefore Rome in modern times, the representative of corrupt Christianity. Clay and its equivalents, *"dust of the ground"* and *"earth"* are used in scripture to depict the natural human state. The natural man is described by Paul as *"of the earth, made of dust"* when contrasted with the spiritual (1 Corinthians 15:47-49). Clay is a symbol of raw human nature that needs to be fashioned by God as the potter (Isaiah 64:8). The clay in Daniel's vision is baked clay. It has not been subject to God's discipline but has come under the influence of human potters. It represents men and women following their own ways completely, and since the image is all about rulership of the earth the clay stands for secular government and society. Since the iron and the clay stand for two groups of people with different values, one religious and one secular, the meaning of the phrase *"the kingdom shall be divided"* begins to come clear.

The fulfilment

> *"The kingdom shall be divided"*

This *"dividing"* occurred during the 19th and early 20th centuries. To understand the process it is best to step back and look first at the period before it happened. Most nations in the area where corrupt Christianity had taken hold were previously deemed to be Christian. There were always two powers, one religious and one secular: Church and State. But the two were officially united, and in this sense the kingdom was one kingdom. During the 19th and 20th centuries they became divided as the secular powers moved away from the Church. Various ideas were having an effect which were based on human thinking rather than Church teaching. These ideas spawned a host of political, philosophical and social movements. So powerful were these movements that, aided by political events, they resulted in the dividing of Church and State, the dividing of the kingdom referred to by Daniel. National governments broke away from the power of the Church and set themselves free to be run on secular, human lines. This 'secularisation of the State' is what the prophecy means when it reveals that the *"the kingdom shall be divided"*.

> *"the strength of the iron shall be in it ... the kingdom shall be partly strong and partly fragile"*

Under the pressure of these events the Church could have caved in to secular thinking but it has shown itself to be a successor of Rome by demonstrating the same iron strength, vigorously maintaining its traditions. But because iron is now only half of the picture the image will only be "partly strong". Since the other half is clay, the image will be "partly fragile". The fragility is enhanced because the clay is baked, making it brittle. (The literal

An example of *"the kingdom shall be divided"*

The relationship of Church and State in France provides an interesting illustration of the changes that took place in the 19th and 20th centuries.

➤ Arising from the spread of Christianity in the 5th and 6th centuries AD the Catholic Church became the official state religion of France.

➤ Following the trend towards secularisation in the 19th century an act was passed by the French Chamber of Deputies called the "Law of 9th December 1905 concerning the separation of the Churches and the State". It divided Church and State with its main objective being summarised in the phrase, "The Republic neither recognises, nor salaries, nor subsidises any religion".

The fact that this act needed to be passed confirms that Church and State were previously aligned and needed to be separated to reflect modern thinking. It is a specific example of Daniel's words, *"the kingdom shall be divided"*.

meaning of the word "fragile" is 'to shatter'.) Thus human thinking will be instrumental in weakening the image in God's sight and hastening its own end.

> "but they will not adhere to one another, just as iron does not mix with clay"

Society has continued to move in the secular direction. The secular trend has been so powerful that it has created a godless society in which there is virtually no support for religion. This has been opposed by the traditional Church which has spoken out against such ideas as women priests and the acceptance of homosexual practices. This clash of ideals between the iron of Church and the clay of secular human society is a fulfilment of the prophecy that *"they will not adhere to one another"*.

> "they will mingle with the seed of men"

In some areas however, the Church, even the traditional wing, has been prepared to accept modern, humanist ideas. The clearest example is the almost universal adoption of human rights. These 'rights' lie at the heart of modern human thinking. The core of Bible teaching of course is that man has no 'rights' but is wholly dependent on the grace of God to meet both his spiritual and material needs. When Daniel uses the phrase, *"they will mingle with the seed of men"*, the original language for "the seed of men" has overtones of marriage. It is

pointing back to the days before the flood when *"the sons of God saw the daughters of men, that they were beautiful; and they took wives for themselves of all whom they chose"* (Genesis 6:2). The *"sons of God"* were those who should have been God's servants but had corrupted godly truth to the point where they felt free to mix with the *"daughters of men"*, that is those who were totally secular. In the last days the same process will be repeated, the adherents of corrupt Christianity will make an accommodation with secular society. The Lord Jesus described the last days as being *"as it was in the days of Noah"*, so there is a consistency here.

What should disciples be watching for?

One writer, describing the papacy at the end of the 20th century has effectively summarised these points:

> "The intellectual climate in the West since the age of revolution has often been hostile to the papacy ... The pontificate of John Paul II reflects the accommodation and confrontation of the papacy with developments from the onset of the French Revolution to the end of the Cold War. Like his predecessors over the past two centuries, the present pope has espoused traditional views on certain matters while seeking accommodation on others." (*The Modern Papacy since 1789* – Frank J. Coppa)

The feet of iron and clay last until the Lord Jesus returns and the kingdom is established. In some things the Church will retain its strength as Daniel predicted and refuse to change its traditional teaching. The book of Revelation confirms that the Church and State will remain separate until the end and the Church will not recover its political power. But, despite the conflict of ideals, the Church will be so successful in *"mingling with the seed of men"* that it will have a position of significant influence at the return of the Lord Jesus. It is watching progress towards this outcome that will prove fascinating for Bible believers.

Disciples and the world around them

Most disciples today live in an environment with a lifestyle and set of values far removed from Bible teaching. Daniel's example sets all of us thinking about how we live. Disciples are in the world like him and should not seek to escape from it. The separation taught by the Lord Jesus is moral, not physical. But a separation there must be. Like Daniel we must firmly make up our minds to turn away from those things which could bring the values of the world into our lives. They will almost certainly influence us and set our minds on a train of thought which is not the mind of Christ. We live in an age which is very clever at invading our lives. If we know something is influencing us in the wrong direction then we must put it behind us and turn to those things that build us up in the faith. Disciples are strengthened by prayerful reading of God's word and working together in fellowship with other believers which always makes it so much easier. We can only imagine how grateful Daniel and his friends were to have each other in those difficult times.

The fiery furnace

DANIEL CHAPTER 3

Nebuchadnezzar sets up a golden image which all his subjects are required to worship. The three friends refuse and are thrown into a fiery furnace. They are delivered by an angel and Nebuchadnezzar glorifies God. It is an example of the impact of belief in the kingdom of God on those who have made it the basis of their lives.

NEBUCHADNEZZAR had received the image dream with great enthusiasm. Unfortunately he may well have missed the point about its purpose. He may have thought the head of gold was designed to portray him as the greatest leader in history. Perhaps it was this that lay behind his setting up the golden image. In any event, he was soon assembling an international gathering to fall down before it in an act of dedication (verses 1,2). It did not necessarily represent Nebuchadnezzar or his gods but it was certainly intended to be a point of worship, a focus for his empire, a means of promoting loyalty to this insecure king (verse 5). To encourage the doubters the penalty for refusing to worship the image was to be cast into a fiercely

burning furnace. Jeremiah confirms that this was a method of punishment in Babylon (Jeremiah 29:22) and excavations have unearthed large brick kilns, capable of being heated to great temperatures which would probably have doubled as a furnace for this very purpose. The encouragement certainly worked on the assembled subjects. The literal translation of verse 7 is, *"as soon as they were hearing it they were falling down"*. They couldn't fall down fast enough before the golden image.

The faith of Shadrach, Meshech and Abed-Nego

We don't know where Daniel was at this time. His three friends were clearly in Babylon although in a precarious position. The rapid promotion of the three young Jewish captives after the image dream had aroused the jealousy of their peers. Their refusal to bow down to the image gave the Chaldeans the chance they had been looking for and they *"maliciously accused the Jews"* (verse 8, ESV). Nebuchadnezzar's fury was great but he had to be seen to be just in front of the international assembly. He gave Shadrach, Meshach and Abed-Nego another chance. Again, their response is a model for all believers under threat. They were polite but firm, completely unwavering. Nebuchadnezzar asked them which god could deliver from his hand. There was never any doubt in their minds that their God was capable of delivering them out of Nebuchadnezzar's hand and they told him so directly. At the same time they accepted that it may not be God's will and they might perish in the flames, but nothing would change their minds (verses 16-18). The king's anger erupted and the friends were thrown into the overheated furnace. But the Lord God knows how to deliver His people from the worst that man can do and they came out of the fire completely unmarked. Once more, the Lord God had chosen to glorify Himself through his servants who trust in Him.

Nebuchadnezzar glorifies God

The deliverance of Shadrach, Meshach and Abed-Nego was described by Nebuchadnezzar himself and is therefore initially couched in the language of the Babylonian religions. He saw the three friends and a fourth *"like a son of the gods"* (verse 25) walking unhurt in the furnace. But it was beyond question an act of God and for the second time in his life the king gave Him the glory through a command that was sent to all corners of his empire. By the time he got round to issuing his decree he had probably had the truth explained to him by the three friends. This time he declared that it was an angel from God who *"delivered His servants who*

trusted in Him" (verse 28). The king was gaining a deeper and better understanding of the God of Israel. He had heard the truth through the interpretation of the image dream; he had seen the Lord God at work in the lives of his followers; he was now ready for a final, key revelation about his own position which is the subject of the next chapter.

Idolatry today

Not many disciples today come under pressure to bow to a golden image. But there are other things to worship that are not right. The Apostle Paul talks about *"covetousness, which is idolatry"* (Colossians 3:5). Materialism is a feature of the last days and believers are pressurised to worship its gods. These idols offer more money, bigger houses, better cars, impressive technology and exotic holidays. Worshipping these is false worship, they are idols with no life in them and they take us away from serving God. Paul shows us the right way: *"having food and clothing, with these we shall be content"* (1 Timothy 6:8).

Why did God deliver the three friends?

It is striking that on the three occasions when Daniel and his friends are persecuted (chapters 1, 3 and 6), God delivers them miraculously. But this is not always the case for God's people. The persecution prophesied in chapter 11 resulted in death for some (verse 33) and Hebrews 11 gives many examples of believers who died for their faith. So what is different about these three incidents in Daniel? They are enacted parables to accompany the prophecies about the kingdom of God. His people find themselves in the kingdom of men and there is an ongoing conflict which can result in persecution. It is the disciples' belief in the coming kingdom that sustains them in trial. It is part of the message of Daniel that God can, and ultimately will deliver His people from the power of Man. These three examples are there to demonstrate that God is more powerful than the greatest in the kingdom of men. *"The Lord is my helper; I will not fear. What can man do to me?"* (Hebrews 13:6).

Nebuchadnezzar's tree dream

DANIEL CHAPTER 4

Nebuchadnezzar has another dream which Daniel interprets. It tells the king he will become ill and lose his empire for a time. It will be returned to him but he will have learned that God is in control of world affairs. He is only the king of Babylon because it is God's will. The dream is used to tell him a second time that man's rule will come to an end.

THE helpful thing about this chapter is that we are left in no doubt about its purpose. It centres on a dream that was given *"in order that the living may know that the Most High rules in the kingdom of men"* (verse 17). This is confirmed by Daniel in his own commentary on what happened (5:18-21). The events took place a long time after the image dream of chapter 2 and there is a significant change in Nebuchadnezzar. He is no longer an insecure, paranoiac king, worried about his place in history. By the time of chapter 4 the Babylonian empire is well established and Nebuchadnezzar has completed a number of magnificent building projects. There is no more lying awake at nights, he is at peace with himself: *"I,* Nebuchadnezzar, was at rest in my house, and flourishing in my palace"* (verse 4). Then he had the dream.

The details of the dream

This time he remembered the details and retold them clearly. He dreamed of a large tree in the middle of the earth, reaching to the heavens and visible to the ends of the known world. It was a fruitful tree, giving shelter and food for all, humans, animals and birds. While the king watched, an angel came from heaven and commanded that the tree be chopped down, its branches and leaves to be stripped. The tree would be reduced to a stump held together with two metal bands, one of iron and one of bronze. This stump left in the grass is identified with an unnamed man who goes through a period of seven years when he behaves like a beast eating the grass. The angel is quite clear about the reason for these dramatic events: it is that those living would see that God is in control of world affairs and sets over the kingdom of men those He wishes, however unsuitable they may be in the eyes of the world.

The interpretation and fulfilment

Daniel was asked to give the interpretation and so for the second time he explains the meaning of a dream to Nebuchadnezzar (verses 19-26). Once he realised what it involved he was understandably nervous about telling the king. He diplomatically adopted the conventions of the day and said, *"If only the dream applied to your enemies"* (verse 19, NIV). The tree of the dream was Nebuchadnezzar himself. As the tree was chopped down, so Nebuchadnezzar would suffer a mental illness leaving him like a beast for seven years. Then normality would return, but with acceptance that God is in control of human affairs. The tree stayed as a stump, giving Nebuchadnezzar assurance that he would again be Babylon's king.

God's purpose in giving Nebuchadnezzar this sober experience was to humble him and bring him to an acceptance of God's authority. He needed to recognise that God was in control of affairs. Daniel urged Nebuchadnezzar to show his acceptance of the Lord God now and make changes in his life. But the king was not easily influenced and he continued in the belief that he, Nebuchadnezzar was responsible for the greatness of Babylon (verses 28-30). So the events happened, just as predicted (verses 31-33).

The importance of the tree stump

Daniel had provided a simple and clear explanation. But there is a secondary teaching which we are left to work out for ourselves. The tree confirmed that Nebuchadnezzar's kingdom would be returned to him after his illness. But why

did it change from something magnificent before Nebuchadnezzar's illness to being a stump afterwards? What had changed? Certainly not Babylon itself, because we read that after his illness Nebuchadnezzar's kingdom was returned to him exactly as it was before (verse 36).

The key to answering these questions is to recognise that this dream parallels the image dream in chapter 2. With the image, Daniel said to Nebuchadnezzar, *"You are this head of gold ..."* In the dream of chapter 4 Daniel said, *"The tree that you saw ... it is you, O king"*. But the head of gold in the image was also the kingdom of men and Nebuchadnezzar was being identified with it as its ruler. So too in chapter 4 the tree is the kingdom of men as well as being Nebuchadnezzar. And as the image continued with succeeding empires represented by various metals until it was destroyed, so the tree would continue with its bands of iron and bronze until it reached its end. The message appears to be the same with both dreams, so what is the difference? It lies in the emphasis and probably results from Nebuchadnezzar's misunderstanding of the image dream. In chapter 4 the emphasis is very much on the end of the kingdom of men, a point which Nebuchadnezzar appears to have missed with the first dream. He noted the image's magnificence and was happy to be the head of gold but overlooked its destruction by the stone, showing the fragility and limited lifespan of the kingdom of men. The tree was initially magnificent

Why no band of silver?

While the tree stump would eventually decay to nothing, it was to be held together for a while by bands of iron and bronze, following the pattern of the image dream of chapter 2. But why not silver to complete the picture of the image? Silver stood for Medo-Persia, the only one of the four empires that did not desecrate the temple, God's dwelling place. We are not told, but this is probably why it does not appear on the tree stump. Desecrating the temple of God is the greatest act of rebellion carried out by the kingdom of men. They are fooling only themselves, thinking that they have triumphed over the Lord God and taken possession of the earth. Babylon, Greece and Rome desecrated the temple at Jerusalem and therefore qualify to be included in this symbol of the tree stump which portrays so well the kingdom of men. The Persians, however, were instrumental in initiating the rebuilding of the temple which is the centre of God's eternal purpose, and they are spared inclusion in this picture of decay.

as well, but this time its end was portrayed much more graphically. A tree stump, even with metal bands around it, would eventually decay and disappear. Nebuchadnezzar was being given the same message a second time but in a way he could not possibly miss. And this understanding would become his salvation. It was because the kingdom of men will one day cease to exist that Nebuchadnezzar needed to change his life to prepare himself for the kingdom of God. The record is quite specific, the kingdom would only be

restored to him **after** he had come to this understanding (4:26,27). What a blessing!

He was being very human. We find it easy to believe that what we see around us is real, permanent and wonderful. It can be hard to appreciate it will one day come to an end. Sometimes it takes a life-changing event, such as Nebuchadnezzar's illness, to get us to accept God's control, produce a humble outlook and renew our focus on preparing for His kingdom. Nebuchadnezzar may have missed the message the first time but nowhere is there any hint of rebuke, just the reverse in fact. The Lord simply gives him a clearer explanation. This is a remarkable chapter. Its purpose is to reveal a fundamental message to all mankind that God rules in the kingdom of men but at the same time shows His care for Nebuchadnezzar in leading him to a better understanding.

What can we learn from the dream?

It also shows God's care for us because the dream was intended for the "living", that is all men and women:

- The *"kingdom of men"* is a phrase found in verses 17, 25 and 32. *"Kingdom"* is always singular, showing there is only one kingdom of men in God's sight. At this time it was ruled over by Babylon but other empires would come after it.
- God rules in this kingdom and gives it to those He chooses. At that particular time He had given it to Nebuchadnezzar but whoever rules

---

Study points

➤ Who was the *"watcher"* (verses 13,17,23)? It was an angel of God because the dream was *"the decree of the Most High"* (verse 24). But the Babylonians would not have understood the word *"angel"* because in their religions they were called *"watchers"*. Nebuchadnezzar was simply using the only word he knew.

➤ *"The lowest of men"* (verse 17). This is a reference to social status, not a character description! Nebuchadnezzar's father had come to the throne and although a respected Chaldean he was not from a family that would normally provide kings. He described himself as the "son of a nobody".

➤ *"Seven times"* (verses 16,23,32). No information is given about the length of a "time" but almost all commentators accept that a period of one year is meant.

➤ Nebuchadnezzar's illness. It used to be thought it was Lycanthropy, a rare illness with symptoms similar to those he experienced. The modern approach is more general, a form of acute insanity.

is there by divine appointment (Jeremiah 27:5,6). The accession to power may appear to be following natural events, but the Bible teaches that the Lord God is working behind the scenes.

- When Nebuchadnezzar was full of pride in his own achievements his heart was changed from a man's to a beast's. What is impressive to men is nothing in God's sight because people have only been following their natural instincts and not giving glory to Him.

- The tree *"reached to the heavens"* in the same way as the Tower of Babel was intended to be a building *"whose top is in the heavens"*. The heavens stand for rulership and this is Man's way of trying to take ownership of the earth from God.

Nebuchadnezzar's closing words

The last we hear of Nebuchadnezzar in the book of Daniel is in the wonderful words of praise in these final verses of this chapter (verses 34-37). They leave us in no doubt that he understood the revelations given him, both the truth about the coming kingdom of God and the impact of that truth on men and women.

 Lessons for disciples

Daniel was preaching to Nebuchadnezzar. Two points are worth noting:

➤ He used the language and idiom that Nebuchadnezzar would understand, such as the word *"watcher"* in verse 23, but never compromised his message. Like Paul he was *"all things to all men"* in the sense that he ensured they would be able to receive the lessons from God's word. But this was done without diluting the message in any way or getting involved in false worship. See also 1 Corinthians 10:32,33.

➤ After preaching about the kingdom, Daniel informed the king about a change in lifestyle (verse 27). It is not just a matter of believing the Gospel of the kingdom, it has to change our lives and the lives of those to whom we preach.

Belshazzar's feast

DANIEL CHAPTER 5

Belshazzar the king

It used to be thought that Belshazzar was Nebuchadnezzar's grandson but recent research has cast doubt on this. Belshazzar's father was Nabonidus who was not descended from Nebuchadnezzar. Nabonidus spent most of his time away from Babylon on campaigns. Belshazzar was left in charge as crown prince although filling the role of king in his father's absence (verse 1). He was therefore the second ruler in the kingdom after his father which explains why he could only appoint a third ruler (verses 7,16,29). References to Nebuchadnezzar being his father (verse 2) are used figuratively; most modern translations have "ancestor" as an alternative.

Exactly as predicted the empire of Babylon comes to an end. At a feast which Belshazzar makes for his lords when he mocks the God of Israel, a message is given to him that makes clear the days of his kingdom are over. By the end of the night the Medes and Persians are in control.

THE Medes and Persians had been closing on Babylon for a while before this fateful night. Because the city was built so well its citizens thought it could never be overrun. Full of confidence Belshazzar laid on a great feast for his lords. Of course they should have been checking the defences as Nebuchadnezzar would have done had he still been alive. But Belshazzar wasn't in the same league as his great predecessor. Neither could he match him in terms of spiritual insight.

The challenge to the Lord God

When Nebuchadnezzar learned in chapter 4 that Daniel's God was the "*King of heaven*" he had publicised the fact. Most important of all Belshazzar knew (5:18-22). This knowledge brought responsibility and he should have genuinely humbled himself.

Instead, in an act of drunken bravado, he challenged the Lord God by drinking out of the cups from the Jerusalem temple. Many such items were taken from peoples in the empire as the Babylonians conquered one nation after another. The fact that Belshazzar so deliberately selected those from Jerusalem suggests that Nebuchadnezzar may have locked them away with instructions that they should not be touched. What Belshazzar did in reality was to declare himself greater than the Lord God, or, in Daniel's words, "*you have lifted yourself up against the Lord of heaven*" (verse 23).

What Belshazzar did not realise, because he had not listened, was that the people of Judah were only under Babylonian rule because their God had made it so and then only for seventy years which were coming to an end. Neither had it penetrated that he was only the ruler of the world because it was God's will. Had he listened to his predecessor he would have known. What he had wilfully ignored was finally made clear in the writing on the wall.

The writing on the wall

The words that appeared in front of Belshazzar may seem to us to be some kind of foreign or even divine language. In fact they were in Aramaic so would have been easily understood by all those present. The problem was in the interpretation and none of the Chaldeans could help. It was the queen who came in to the feast and drew attention to Daniel. She was not one of Belshazzar's wives as they were already present (verse 2). Probably she was his mother who would have remembered Daniel from the days of Nebuchadnezzar. Once again Daniel was called to the king's presence to interpret God's message. The words are Mene, Mene, Tekel, Upharsin. The first two words are identical and are repeated which is the mark of divine emphasis (Genesis 41:32). The 'U' in front of Pharsin simply means 'and'. The three words are all words associated with weights and sometimes with currency.

Mene

The associated word is *mina,* a measure of weight from which Daniel derives the verb 'numbered' or 'appointed'. God had set a time limit on Belshazzar's kingdom and the limit had been reached. The number was seventy, the same as the years of Judah's exile (Jeremiah 25:11,12).

Tekel

Associated with shekel, a unit of weight and currency. Daniel used the verbal form, 'weighed' or 'assessed'. Belshazzar had been weighed in the balances and found wanting.

He had not responded to God's revelation to Nebuchadnezzar and he openly rebelled against the Lord God, the final act of iniquity which was responsible for Babylon's downfall.

Pharsin

This is a plural noun. The singular is *peres* which means 'part' or 'half'. Used as a verb by Daniel it became 'shared' or 'divided'. That is, the kingdom would be shared amongst the Medes and Persians.

Surprisingly, and presumably under the influence of the wine, Belshazzar took no notice of the impending doom and rewarded Daniel as he had promised. But the end was inevitable and, that same night, as Daniel had foretold so long ago, the empire of Babylon became the empire of the Medes and the Persians.

The importance of Belshazzar's feast

This chapter's events are included in the book because they are an essential part of Daniel's message:

- What the Lord God says about the future always comes true.
- He is wholly in control of events on earth and decides who is to govern at any time.
- World events are moving steadily but firmly towards the kingdom of God.

Who was Darius the Mede?

Daniel states that Darius the Mede took over the kingdom (verse 31). The problem is that the historical records of the Persian empire do not support this. They show that Cyrus was the king when Babylon was overthrown. It is now believed that Darius and Cyrus were one and the same person:

➤ Daniel 6:28 apparently records both kings, but the original word for "and" can also be translated "even". This makes them the same person.

➤ Cyrus' mother was a Mede and his father a Persian, so he could legitimately be called a Mede.

➤ The Old Testament was translated into Greek only a few centuries after these events and it has Cyrus instead of Darius.

The lions' den

DANIEL CHAPTER 6

Daniel is promoted by Darius to a very senior position in the kingdom. This arouses the jealousy of his colleagues. They attempt to have him removed from office by making it illegal for him to worship his God. Daniel refuses to comply and Darius is forced to put him in the lions' den. God delivers Daniel and the king honours the God of Israel.

NO ONE was more aware than Darius the king that this was an age of corruption in high places. In this murky environment Daniel shone like a star and his integrity brought him to one of the three highest positions, *"so that the king would suffer no loss"* (verse 2). Even among these three he stood out clearly and Darius let it be known he was thinking of promoting Daniel to be governor over the whole empire. The expressions used about Daniel in the first five verses are a testimony to his godly character. He *"distinguished himself above the governors ... because an excellent spirit was in him ... they could find no charge or fault, because he was faithful, nor was there any error or fault found in him ... 'We shall not find any charge against this Daniel unless we find it against him concerning the law of his God'".*

The opposition of his peers

The prospect of Daniel being promoted over them all was the last straw for his fellow ministers. It may have been jealousy or simply the prospect of some honest accounting. They realised the only way to bring Daniel down in Darius' eyes was to use his religion. A simple plot was hatched. Darius would be asked to sign a decree banning petitions to any god or man except the king for thirty days. The penalty for disobedience was to be thrown to the lions. The king may have welcomed the idea as a way of fostering loyalty among the subjects of his widespread empire. He signed the decree, apparently in ignorance of the implications.

Daniel, aware of the new law, went home and prayed three times that same day. This would have been morning, noon and evening (Psalm 55:16,17). It was clearly something he did regularly as his enemies seemed to know of his habit. What did he pray about? Since he faced Jerusalem (verse 10) we can deduce that he prayed for forgiveness for the Jews, fulfilling the Lord's command to his people in exile (2 Chronicles

6:36-39). But we can also be sure that on this particular day the prayer was personal and a man of such faith would have brought his precarious position to the Father in trust.

Saved from the lions

But it was a very public prayer and there was no shortage of 'observers' to take good note. Darius was devastated when the facts were reported. He worked for the rest of the day, presumably with the best lawyers to find a way round the decree. But to his consternation the king was left with no choice and the law had to take its course – Daniel was put in the lions' den. What emerged in the hours that followed was the tremendous affection that Darius had for Daniel and his awareness that Daniel's whole life revolved around his service to God. The king spent the night fasting and hurried in the dawn light to the mouth of the den. To his great joy Darius discovered that Daniel's God had indeed saved him and he was brought out unharmed. The inspired statement that Daniel was saved *"because he believed in his God"* (verse 23) is echoed in the New Testament where he is held up as an example of faith, *"who through faith ... stopped the mouths of lions"* (Hebrews 11:33). It was an enacted parable of resurrection. Daniel had been placed in a pit which was to become his grave. Not even the mightiest ruler and all the laws of this world could save him from death. It was only his faith in the power and grace of God which gave him life.

The effect on the king

Darius reminds us of Nebuchadnezzar in the command issued to the peoples of his empire (verses 25-27). Clearly Daniel had been hard at work preaching to the king whose decree shows a remarkable grasp of the Truth. He speaks of the *"living God"* (in contrast to the lifeless idols around him) and of the kingdom and dominion that will last for ever.

The believer and the world

➤ Daniel was held in great esteem and affection by those in the world around him. It applied from the beginning of his exile (1:9) to Darius (6:14) over seventy years later. He was like the Lord Jesus who increased *"in favour with God and men"*. Such favour follows from putting into practice the Lord's teaching of love and humility in dealings with others. Paul exhorts us *"to speak evil of no one, to be peaceable, gentle, showing all humility to all men"* (Titus 3:2).

➤ But in a world that doesn't know the Lord God it is possible we may find ourselves in conflict with it, like Daniel. We might lose our job, or our beliefs may place us on the wrong side of the law. Situations like this call for the message of Daniel that gives support and direction. We live for the kingdom of God and are *"strangers and pilgrims"* in this present age, knowing it will pass away. *"Therefore let us go forth to him, outside the camp, bearing his reproach. For here we have no continuing city, but we seek the one to come"* (Hebrews 13:13,14). We serve a Father who cares for all His children and whose angel *"encamps all around those who fear Him"*, like Daniel, who was delivered *"because he believed in his God"*.

The vision of the four beasts

DANIEL CHAPTER 7

This is the second of the four prophecies. Daniel has a vision of four beasts which correspond to the empires of the image dream. More detail is given of the fourth empire and its impact on Gentile disciples. A power will arise from it that will be in opposition to God and will persecute His people. But the end will come with the destruction of the beast and the establishment of the kingdom of God.

GIVEN at the beginning of Belshazzar's reign, about 552 BC, the vision follows a similar pattern to the first prophecy in chapter 2. We see again the four empires that are to affect God's people, this time with a particular focus on the fourth. The empires are symbolised as beasts. Instead of the magnificent image of a man we see the kingdoms as they are perceived in heaven – men following their own instincts rather than God's will.

The setting of the vision

It was a vision of the night, the darkness characterising a world in the grip of the kingdom of men. Lying on his bed, Daniel became an observer of events that were to affect God's people until the kingdom is established. He was not alone, but angels were also watching and it is one of these who answers Daniel's questions. The chapter breaks down into two main sections:

- Verses 2-14,21,22: the record of events which Daniel observed and wrote down directly. These are prefixed by "*I saw*" or "*I looked*" and similar phrases.
- Verses 15-20,23-27: a conversation with one of the angels where Daniel asks questions about the vision and receives explanations.

The setting of the vision is a sea with four winds blowing on it:

- The sea is the 'Great Sea' which would have been the Mediterranean for the people of Daniel's time. All of the empires touched it at some point. But since the focus of the vision is the fourth kingdom, it was particularly relevant as the Roman empire was established around the Mediterranean.
- Winds blew from the four points of the compass. Winds in the Bible can be used to symbolise human ideas and political manoeuvring (Ephesians 4:14). It is this human ambition which

is signified here, driving men to expand and conquer other lands.

Daniel observed four beasts arising **from the sea** (verse 3) which describes the setting of the vision as men see it. But the angel described the beasts as arising from the earth (verse 17) confirming that, viewed from heaven, the empires make up the kingdom of men which has an earthly rather than a heavenly character. In that same verse the angel explains that the beasts represent kings, but later confirms that this means a kingdom or empire (verse 23). The beasts were a lion, a bear, a leopard and an animal that does not exist in the natural world.

The first three beasts

As this vision is primarily intended for disciples affected by the fourth beast we are not told a great deal about the first three. More detail is given about them in later visions in Daniel; what we are told is sufficient to identify them.

The lion (verse 4) has eagle's wings which are removed; it then stands up like a man and is given a man's heart. When the word 'man' is used in Daniel it normally represents mankind in opposition to the things of God. The standing up reflects the image of chapter 2 where Babylon is the empire at the point when the image is erected to stand on its feet. We are told that *"a man's heart was given to it"*, depicting the self-confidence that characterises the kingdom of men (e.g. Nebuchadnezzar – 4:30,37). This beast

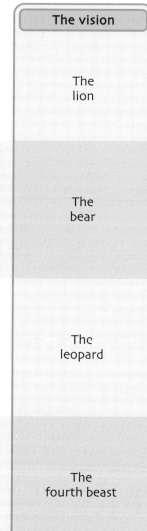
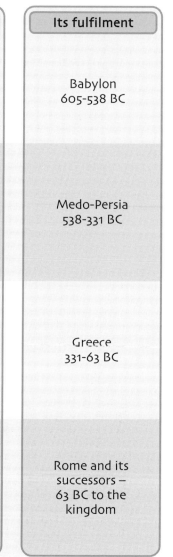

The vision	Its fulfilment
The lion	Babylon 605-538 BC
The bear	Medo-Persia 538-331 BC
The leopard	Greece 331-63 BC
The fourth beast	Rome and its successors – 63 BC to the kingdom

represents Babylon, the first of the four empires constituting the kingdom of men from the time of Daniel onwards. But the symbol clearly has two phases, the first with eagle's wings and the second when it stands up like a man. Jeremiah explains the two phases: *"Israel is like scattered sheep; the lions have driven him away. First the king of Assyria devoured him; now at last this Nebuchadnezzar king of Babylon has broken his bones"* (Jeremiah 50:17).

The bear (verse 5) has the particular feature of being raised up on one side. By the time the Medes and Persians took over from Babylon the Persians had become the dominant partner. The three ribs represent the three divisions of the Persian empire we have already met in chapter 6 (verse 2). The Persians were destined to conquer a vast area but there was to be some resistance from one of the emperors at a key point. The angels observing with Daniel had to intervene to encourage this emperor to *"devour much flesh"*. (We see the angels dealing with this resistance later in 10:13.)

The leopard (verse 6) is known for its speed of movement and sudden attacks. The accounts of Alexander the Great and his conquests show why this symbol has been chosen for the Greeks. The leopard has four wings on its back, and four heads. The multiple wings emphasise the immense speed of the Greek armies storming across the Middle East. The four heads capture the successive political structures of Greece leading up to and including the prophecy: (1) the city states, (2) a confederacy under Philip of Macedon, (3) a united nation under Alexander the Great, (4) the military hierarchies that followed Alexander.

The fourth beast

Much more is told us about the empire of the fourth beast:

1 It is the fourth kingdom, different from all the beasts before it, different from all other kingdoms (verses 7,19,23).

2 It is dreadful and terrible, exceedingly strong, devouring the whole earth, trampling it and breaking it in pieces (verses 7,19,23).

An everyday fulfilment of prophecy

After AD 70 only a few Jews remained in the Roman province of Judaea. Even so, they rebelled again in AD 132 under Bar-Kochba. This time the Romans decided to end the Jewish problem once and for all. The revolt was brutally suppressed, Jews were killed or deported and villages were razed to the ground. The Romans were so thorough in exterminating the Jewish presence that the provinces of Judaea, Samaria and Galilee were erased from Roman maps. Short of ideas for a new name, they turned as ever to the Greeks who called the land Syria Palaestina after the Greek word for the Philistines. This is the origin of the name Palestine, familiar to us today. It is an example of the Roman thoroughness prophesied by Daniel in the words, *"breaking in pieces and trampling the residue with its feet"* (verses 7,19), and the adoption of the Greek culture symbolised in the nails of bronze. Every day when we hear of Palestine in the media we are reminded of the accuracy of God's word.

---

3   It has huge iron teeth and nails of bronze (verses 7,19).

4   It develops ten horns which are ten kings arising from the original kingdom (verses 7,20,24).

5   After the ten horns have arisen, a little horn will come up among them, before whom three of the first horns will be plucked out by the roots. It will be different from the first horns. It will have eyes like the eyes of a man and a mouth speaking blasphemous words against God. Its appearance will be greater than its fellows. It will make war against the saints and prevail against them. The saints will be given into its hand for "*a time, times and a half*". It will intend to change times and law. Its dominion will be taken away at the judgement (verses 8,20,21,24,25).

6   The beast will be slain, its body destroyed and given to the burning flame (verse 11).

1. It is a fourth kingdom

We can identify the fourth beast easily since Rome was the kingdom that followed Greece. It was marked out in the vision as being different from the other empires in the complete and thorough way it was to govern. It gradually came to power in the centuries before Christ, conquered almost all of the known world and held it in an iron grip for six hundred years. It had great political skills and military might. Such was the impact of this empire that its legacy is still with us today; no other empire has left such a mark on history.

2. It will be exceedingly dreadful

These characteristics of the beast are parallel to the description of the legs of iron in chapter 2 (verse 40). The Romans were quite clever in the way they managed conquered peoples whom they aimed to get on their side. But when opposition arose they were merciless and their approach to dealing with any who stood against them could not be described better than these words in Daniel 7. One of the best known examples is when the Jewish people revolted in AD 70. Four Roman legions were assembled to crush the rebellion which they did ruthlessly. They focused on Jerusalem, finally destroying it

Animals as symbols

Scripture uses animals as symbols and they are often given features such as a number of horns or heads. We can make a distinction between these. A horn represents a political power. An animal can have more than one horn at the same time. So, a set of horns depicts a number of powers existing alongside each other at the same time. A head represents a way of thinking, that is, a type of government such as dictatorship or democracy. But in the same way that an animal can only have one head, a nation can only have one type of government at any one time. So a number of heads on an animal symbolises successive types of government, i.e. they come one after the other, each with something different about them. Where, for example, an empire goes from dictatorship to democracy it would be symbolised by two heads, but it would be fulfilled in practice by one following the other. A good example of the use of these symbols is Revelation 17:7-13 where the ten horns represent nations existing alongside each other but the seven heads stand for successive kings or types of government.

including the temple. Thousands of Jews were killed, many fled and the Romans enslaved those they captured.

3. It has huge iron teeth and nails of bronze

A creature such as this holds its prey in its claws and devours it with its teeth. Both are given to us as part of the symbolism, using the iron and bronze metals of the image in chapter 2. The secret of Rome's success was the efficiency of its army; the "iron teeth". It was disciplined, highly trained and well equipped. This single-minded military machine made the Romans successful in "devouring" those peoples they set out to conquer.

Roman society was not so strong in philosophy, culture and sport. For these they simply turned to the Greeks who excelled in them, so providing the Roman beast with "nails of bronze". A poet of the time wrote, "Captive Greece took her wild captor captive". By the time of the Lord Jesus, Greek culture was the accepted standard.

The Lord Jesus would have seen clearly the fulfilment of this prophecy. All around him his people were held in the bronze claws of Greek culture and about to be devoured by the iron teeth of the mighty Roman army in AD 70.

4. It develops ten horns

The original empire based on Rome came to an end around AD 500. But as with the image of chapter 2, the prophecy makes it clear that the fourth kingdom continues until the kingdom of God is established. The ten horns refer to the breaking up of the empire as Rome lost its grip. In AD 330 the emperor Constantine moved his headquarters from Rome to Constantinople. This sowed the seeds of a split in the empire between east and west. During the period AD 400-600 the western half (broadly West Europe) was overrun by barbarian tribes who took advantage of Rome's increasing weakness. These tribes are symbolised by the ten horns. History books vary on the number of tribes, some suggesting slightly

---

The fourth beast and the other empires

This vision in chapter 7 develops the theme that the whole kingdom of men will be represented at the time of the end.

➤ it is the fourth beast that is destroyed but the other empires also exist because we are told that *"their lives were prolonged for a season and a time"* (7:12). It must mean that the modern successors of the previous empires will be present.

➤ this agrees with the image prophecy as we have already seen. The empires in the image will be *"crushed together"* (2:35), that is, the modern equivalents of the various empires portrayed by the image will be present at the time of the end.

➤ the fourth beast will have *"nails of bronze"* introducing the idea that while it is Rome it will also contain characteristics of the previous empires.

This suggests that the first three beasts are in some way merged into the fourth. Now count up the total of the number of heads on the four beasts in Daniel 7 and then read Revelation 13:1,2!

---

less than ten and some more. The prophecy has to deal with these changing divisions of the empire over a long period of time and so gives us a number reflecting an 'average' of what was to happen during those years. We must remember the vision is symbolic and is not writing detailed history in advance. What is important is that the barbarian tribes were great admirers of Rome, seeing themselves as inheritors, not destroyers of the empire. This continuation of what Rome had created was reflected in the western half of the empire with the establishing of the Holy Roman Empire in AD 800. It finalised the split between east and west. The Holy Roman Empire was a merging of religious and secular powers. It lasted until the 19th century when Church and State became divided as foretold by Daniel in the iron and clay of the image prophecy. The book of Revelation completes the picture, taking this fourth beast of Daniel 7 and supplying more detail. At the time of the end, the ten horns of the beast will exist in a clearly recognisable form for a brief period; they will unite and oppose the Lord Jesus when he returns (Revelation 17:12-14).

5. A little horn

Some time after the ten horns arose, a little horn appeared, looming large in the prophecy and is therefore clearly important. It is a horn so has political power like the ten, confirmed by its taking over three of the original horns. But we are told it will be different from the others, since it has *"eyes like the eyes of a man"*, speaking

"pompous words against the Most High" (verses 8,24,25). The use of the word "man" in Daniel normally indicates rebellion against God and that applies here as the horn is speaking against the Lord God, even to the point where it intends to *"change times and law"*. This certainly makes it different from the other horns who were just political powers. So, what are we told to help us identify the little horn?

- It arises out of the fourth beast, so it originates in Rome.
- It is a horn, so will have political power.
- It speaks words against the Lord God, indicating something more than just a political power; it will operate in the religious arena. Since the statements are against God they must be out of line with Bible teaching.
- It arises after the ten horns have taken over the original Roman empire, that is, after AD 600.
- It will persecute God's people.
- Once it has come into being it will exist as a significant, recognisable power until the kingdom of God is established.

For a second time we are directed to the Catholic Church as leader of corrupt Christianity. The Papacy arose gradually as the Bishop of Rome took on a principal role within the Church but it is generally accepted that Pope Gregory the Great was the first real pope, reigning from AD 590-604. After this time the papacy became steadily more identifiable. It was

The 'eyes like the eyes of a man'

This is one of the features of the little horn but what does it mean? It helps to look first at the opposite; the way God looks on the earth, given to us in the vision in chapter 10. These are *"eyes like torches of fire"* (10:6), that is, when God looks on the world He sees the kingdom of men which will be consumed and give way to the kingdom of God. There is a passage in Peter's second letter which gives the practical outworking of this principle (2 Peter 3:10-13). Note from Peter that believers should follow the divine example, that is, they are 'looking for' the end of this present world and they 'look for' the new heavens and earth which is the kingdom of God. When disciples look at world events they see God's purpose working towards its magnificent conclusion. The little horn however, not making use of the insight that Daniel gives, sees a world that will last for ever and makes its pronouncements accordingly. It is therefore speaking *"words **against** the Most High"* (7:25).

instrumental in setting up the Holy Roman Empire in AD 800 and it gained political power, both of which lasted until the 19th century. Daniel tells us that God's people will be put in its power and this means primarily Gentile disciples of the Lord Jesus. For centuries the Catholic Church persecuted those who held different beliefs, using political influence through instruments like the Spanish Inquisition. These persecutions must have been hard to bear, but their foretelling by Daniel would have been a source of great support for the faithful. Daniel tells us the period during which this active persecution would take place was limited to a *"time, times and a half"* (verse 25). A "time" is normally held to be one year, so 3.5 years are spoken of here, or 1260 days (36 months, each of 30 days). Time periods in scripture are often interpreted on the 'day-for-a-year principle' (see alongside), so this one would indicate 1260 years. The persecution ended in the early 19th century, so 1260 years before that takes us to the early days of the Catholic Church. The little horn's opposition to God's people, together with the "pompous words", are instrumental in its destruction when the judgement takes place (verses 11,22). Believers at the time of the end should look for the little horn to be in a prominent position and watch for the great pronouncements that Daniel found so riveting (verse 11).

The judgement and the kingdom

There is a problem with the verses about the judgement and the establishment of the kingdom (verses 9-14,18,27). At first sight the "Ancient of Days" is the Lord God. But He is sitting in judgement (verses 9,10) and we know that the Lord Jesus will be the judge. If the Lord Jesus is the Ancient of Days, who is the "one like the Son of Man" who is brought to him (verse 13)? Again, we need to remember that the vision is symbolic, designed to teach principles, not give practical details about the judgement. The key to understanding these verses is to recognise that there is a perfect unity between God and the Lord Jesus, who has always been the perfect manifestation of His Father. In this sense the title "Ancient of Days" can be applied to both, although the Bible is careful to make a distinction between them. Of the Lord God it says, *"from everlasting to everlasting, You are God"* (Psalm 90:2), and of the Lord Jesus it says, *"whose origin is from of old, from ancient days"* (Micah 5:2, ESV). Perhaps the simplest thing is to allow scripture to provide its own commentary. Read Matthew 16:27, 2 Thessalonians 1:3-10, Revelation 18:8 and Psalm 2:2, all of which speak of the time of the end.

God owns the judgement but it will be carried out by the Lord Jesus, both acting in perfect unity, and Daniel 7 does not distinguish between them. When the judgement is completed the Lord Jesus will receive the kingdom with his disciples: *"Then the kingdom and dominion, and the greatness of the kingdoms under the whole heaven, shall be given to the people, the saints of the Most High. His kingdom is an everlasting kingdom, and all dominions shall serve and obey him"* (verse 27).

Conclusion

This is a powerful prophecy, primarily about the impact of Rome on the Gentile world after the time of the Lord Jesus. We can understand how Daniel felt at the end when he said, *"As for me, Daniel, my thoughts greatly troubled me"*. He was starting to realise that God's purpose was going to continue for a long time. But if this was about the Gentiles, what was to happen to Israel? That question, so vital to Daniel, was answered in the next chapter.

The day-for-a-year principle

Here are two examples of scriptural passages which provide the basis for this method of interpreting time periods:

➤ Israel remaining in the wilderness for forty years, corresponding to the number of days they spied out the land (Numbers 14:34).

➤ As a sign to Israel Ezekiel had to lie on his side for a number of days, which represented *"the years of their iniquity"* (Ezekiel 4:4-6).

Daniel in the letters to Thessalonica

The Apostle Paul visited Thessalonica once, for a preaching campaign (Acts 17:1-9). Though only there for a short time, it is clear that as well as preaching the Gospel he spent time with the new disciples studying the book of Daniel. We know this because later in his first letter to them he refers to *"the times and the seasons"* which he must have explained so thoroughly he didn't need to go over it again (1 Thessalonians 5:1). The phrase *"the times and the seasons"* comes from the book of Daniel (2:21). When Paul wrote to the Thessalonians a second time he reminded them of what he taught them during his visit. There is little doubt that this teaching was based on Daniel 7. Compare the points he makes with what we have discovered:

2 Thessalonians	Daniel 7
Details of the judgement (1:7-10 and 2:8)	Details of the judgement (verses 9-14)
The *"falling away"* and the *"man of sin"*, *"who opposes and exalts himself above all that is called God … so that he sits as God in the temple of God, showing himself that he is God"* (2:3,4)	*"Eyes like the eyes of a man"*; *"shall speak pompous words against the Most High"* (verses 8 and 25)
The *"mystery of lawlessness"* and the *"lawless one"* (2:7,8)	*"He … shall intend to change times and law"* (verse 25)

The *"falling away"* Paul warns about (2 Thessalonians 2:3) is the Greek word *apostasia*, from which we get 'apostasy' – a word used to describe corrupt Christianity. He is telling the Thessalonians that the Lord Jesus will not return until the false Christianity he spoke of elsewhere has arisen (Acts 20:29-31). This apostasy will centre on the *"man of sin"* and last until the time of the end, when it will be destroyed by the Lord Jesus at his second coming (2 Thessalonians 2:8). We suggest that the *"man of sin"* is false Christianity, specifically the institution of the Papacy which was to arise some 600 years after the Apostle Paul wrote this letter and which confirms our understanding of the little horn of Daniel 7. One thing is clear from Paul's use of Daniel: the book is as relevant to disciples of the Lord Jesus as it was to believers in Daniel's own time.

The evening – morning vision

DANIEL CHAPTER 8

> Chapters 8 and 9 contain the third of the four prophecies. Chapter 8 is a vision of the empires but this time with the focus on Israel. It foretells the desecration of Jerusalem in AD 70 and the subsequent desolation of the land for 2,000 years. It introduces the sacrifice of the Lord Jesus which is finally explained in chapter 9. Daniel has to learn that many years are to pass before the kingdom of God will be established.

ELAM was a province of Persia. Shushan was its capital and the site of the Persian emperor's palace. Daniel may have been there on a diplomatic mission on behalf of Belshazzar. The end of Babylon's rule was in sight and so the vision began with Medo-Persia before moving on to Greece and Rome. New details of the empires are given, telling Daniel about their impact on Israel. The language therefore returns to Hebrew at this point. As with the other prophecies, we are taken right through to the time of the end.

The vision was not easy for Daniel to understand and it had to be explained to him by an angel, the explanation beginning in this chapter and completing in chapter 9. The chapter breaks down into two main sections:

- the vision (verses 3-14)
- the first part of the angel's explanation (verses 15-26)

The second part of the explanation is found in 9:20-27.

The empires

Daniel found himself on the banks of the river Ulai in Shushan, originally a canal flowing into the Tigris. Looking up he saw four animals:

1 a ram
2 a he-goat with a large horn
3 the he-goat with four large horns
4 the he-goat with a little horn

These represented succeeding empires from Medo-Persia to the time of the end.

The Ram stood for Medo-Persia (verses 3,4,20). It had two horns representing the initially separate kingdoms of the Medes and the Persians. However, in the very year of this vision Cyrus had finally taken control of the Medes making Persia the dominant partner. This is reflected in the two horns of the ram with the one to come up last (the Persians) reaching higher than the first (the Medes). The ram pushed in all directions of the compass. None could stand against him. This is an exact description of how the Persian empire expanded, especially under Cyrus, to create the largest state the world had yet seen. Lasting for 200 years this empire was finally overthrown by the power described by the next symbol.

The He-goat with the large horn stood for Greece under Alexander the Great (verses 5-7,21). Uniting the Greek states behind him he came from the west and sped across the Middle East. He is credited with being one of the few military commanders in history who never lost a battle. Between 334 and 331 BC Alexander defeated the Persian king Darius III in a number of battles. After the last, when Alexander had captured the Persian royal family, Darius offered a ransom of 10,000 talents to get them back. Alexander refused, an example of the words of this prophecy that he "cast him down to the ground and trampled him". He died unexpectedly in 323 BC when only thirty-two and at the height of his powers. It would have been no surprise to Daniel who had been told, "when he became strong, the large horn was broken" (verse 8).

The He-goat with four large horns represents the Greek empire after the death of Alexander (verses 8,22). There being no obvious successor (Alexander's son was very young), the issue was finally resolved after the battle of Ipsus in 301 BC when the empire was divided into four parts, each under a general:

1   Seleucus ruled in Mesopotamia and Persia.
2   Ptolemy ruled in the Levant and Egypt.
3   Cassander ruled in Macedon.
4   Lysimachus ruled in Thrace.

This is symbolised in the vision by the four large horns that emerged after the large horn, fulfilling the prophecy that they will be "not with its power", i.e. the division of the empire left it much weaker than the original.

The He-goat with a little horn growing out of one of the four stood for Rome (verses 9-12,23-25). During the period of the four Greek states symbolised by the four horns Rome was gradually developing as a power. The Greek states became weaker and the Romans began to annexe Greek territory which was instrumental in the development of the Roman empire. The Seleucid state (no.1 above) which was situated in the area we call Syria ruled peoples to the south and east including Israel. The state was torn by internal factions making it weak. It had slackened its grip on many of the subject territories including the land of the Jews. The Romans effectively took over and in 64 BC the Roman general Pompey occupied himself with restoring order in the Seleucid territories, conducting expeditions to regain control that the Seleucids had lost. The

The symbolic death and resurrection

In verse 18 Daniel goes through a symbolic death and resurrection. It is an enacted parable found elsewhere in scripture. We see it in the life of Abraham (Genesis 15:12), the Apostle John (Revelation 1:17) and Daniel again in chapter 10. In this chapter it taught Daniel of his mortality. He would die before the establishment of the kingdom and would be dependent on God's grace and the saving work of his Messiah to be resurrected at the time of the end.

Romans were therefore growing "*toward the south, toward the east, and toward the Glorious Land*" as Daniel predicted (verse 9). Pompey invaded Israel in 63 BC which is how the Romans came to be there in the time of Christ. So, out of one of the four horns of the goat, the Seleucid kingdom, a "little horn", that is, Rome, arose to conquer Israel. (Note that this little horn represents the whole Roman empire and should not be confused with the little horn of chapter 7 which is just one element of Rome.)

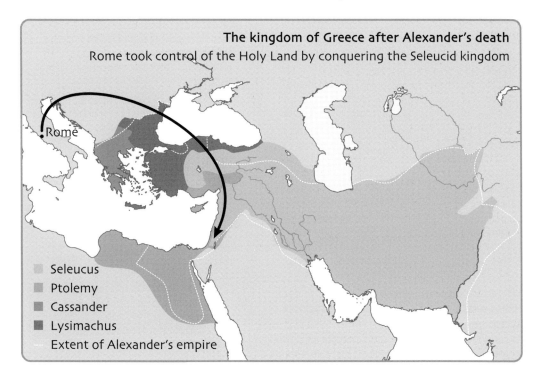

The kingdom of Greece after Alexander's death
Rome took control of the Holy Land by conquering the Seleucid kingdom

- Seleucus
- Ptolemy
- Cassander
- Lysimachus
- Extent of Alexander's empire

The role of the little horn

The little horn triumphed over Israel because it was God's will; it was "*not by his own power*" (verse 24). Both the vision itself (verses 9-12) and the angel's explanation (verses 23-26) focus on Rome from its first involvement with Israel to the desolation of the land after AD 70. But the explanation also goes through to the time of the end, so some of the details in verses 23-26 have a dual fulfilment, applying to the Roman empire **and** to corrupt Christianity in the centuries following. Putting together the details of the vision itself and the angel's explanation we are told about:

1. Rome and the Jews.

> "... having fierce features ... his power shall be mighty ... he shall destroy fearfully ... he shall destroy many in their prosperity ... who understands sinister schemes ...'

These were the characteristics of Roman government: strength, ruthlessness and political skill. Most of them we have already met in the first two prophecies (2:40 and 7:7,19,23).

> "... he even exalted himself as high as the Prince of the host ... he shall even rise against the Prince of princes ... he shall exalt himself in his heart ..."

The Romans crucified the Lord Jesus who was the Prince of the host. Although not realising it, they were rebelling against his Father.

> "... when the transgressors have reached their fullness ..."

It was actually the Jews who brought the Lord Jesus to the Romans to have him crucified. They were the instigators, driven by envy and fear. With this act, their disobedience reached its climax. The Lord had said, *"Fill up, then, the measure of your fathers' guilt"* (Matthew 23:32) and it was this final transgression that triggered the events of AD 70 (Matthew 21:38-41).

> "... it grew up to the host of heaven; and it cast down some of the host and some of the stars to the ground, and trampled them ... he shall destroy the mighty, and also the holy people ..."

The Jews rebelled against Roman rule in AD 70. As the Romans acted swiftly and harshly to put down the rebellion, many of them were killed by the Romans or scattered round the world, leaving only a small number in the land. It was a fulfilment of Deuteronomy 28 (verses 15,49,50,62) that foretold what would happen to Israel if they were disobedient (see also Jesus' words in Matthew 24:29). The host of heaven and the stars here represent the Jewish people, particularly their leaders.

> "... by him the daily sacrifices were taken away, and the place of his sanctuary was cast down. Because of transgression, an army was given over to the horn to oppose the daily sacrifices; and he cast truth down to the ground ..."

After they had crushed the rebellion the Romans destroyed Jerusalem and the temple (Matthew 24:1,2). The word for sanctuary simply means the temple. The daily sacrifices, central to worship under the Law of Moses, ceased. The Hebrew for "daily" is *tamid* which means continual. It refers to the burnt offerings, sacrificed every morning and every evening, that here become a symbol for the whole Law of Moses – the Truth that was brought down.

> "... he did all this and prospered ... and shall prosper and thrive ..."

The little horn, despite the enormity of its rebellion against the Lord God, was not taken away but allowed to prosper.

> "... the transgression of desolation, the giving of both the sanctuary and the host to be trampled underfoot ..."

This is the desolation of Israel. Very few Jews were left in the land after AD 70. For 2,000 years it was occupied and fought over by various powers and faiths until the Jewish people returned in the 20th century,

The 2,300 days (verses 13,14)

One angel asks another how long the vision will last. From the context we take this to refer to the period of desolation in the land of Israel following the events of AD 70. The time period given in response is 2,300 days. The word for "days" is unusual, being 'evening mornings' as in verse 26, and refers to the daily sacrifices offered each evening and morning. Assuming the day-for-a-year principle applies, we are looking at a period of 2,300 years. The Jews regained Jerusalem in 1967 during the Six-Day War. 2,300 years before that takes us to the time when Alexander the Great took over from the Persians (332 BC). This may be significant since it could be that this time period starts with the he-goat. But as with most of the time periods in Daniel, it is not easy to be certain about the starting event and date and this is offered simply as one possible interpretation.

finally recapturing Jerusalem in 1967. The word for sanctuary used here is different from the word found in verse 11. It is more general and includes the land or people.

2. Corrupt Christianity.

> *"... he shall destroy fearfully, and shall prosper and thrive ... he shall destroy the mighty, and also the holy people ... he shall destroy many in their prosperity ... through his cunning he shall cause deceit to prosper under his rule ... he shall exalt himself in his heart ..."*

From what we have already discovered we can apply these words to corrupt Christianity. They are features we recognise, including the persecution of disciples and the promotion of teaching which is full of "deceit" or out of line with the Bible truth (7:8,20,21,25; 2 Thessalonians 2:4).

3. The time of the end.

> *"... he shall even rise against the Prince of princes; but he shall be broken without human means ... the vision refers to the time of the end ... what shall happen in the latter time of the indignation; for at the appointed time the end shall be ... seal up the vision, for it refers to many days in the future"*

So the vision takes us right through to the time of the end when the little horn will be broken, but not by human power. This is the same as the destruction of the image in chapter 2 that will be destroyed by a stone *"cut out without hands"* (2:34), that is, it will be God's work and not man's. It will be fulfilled by the Lord Jesus Christ at his second coming (Matthew 21:42-44; 1 Corinthians 15:23-28). It also confirms that Rome, the final empire, will exist not only in the first century AD, but also at the return of the Lord Jesus when it will oppose him. But in this vision we are not given any details about what form the empire will take at the time of the end.

The purpose of the vision

We shall now go back and look at verses 13-19 which help us identify the purpose of the vision. It is described as the vision *"concerning the daily sacrifices"* (verse 13). This is confirmed by the angel Gabriel who calls it the *"vision of the evenings and mornings"* (verse 26), that is, the daily sacrifices. We must note this description. Sometimes the chapter is referred to as the Vision of the Ram and the He-goat, but that is not what we are told. The angel's description focuses our minds on the ending of the sacrifices and the surrounding events. There are two things in the vision that stand out as reasons why the angel should draw our attention to the taking away of the daily sacrifices. Both of them were apparently new to Daniel:

- The sacrifice of the Lord Jesus: this made unnecessary the daily sacrifices under the law.

- The Roman destruction of the temple and the desolation of Israel

The sacrifice of the Lord Jesus

Daniel was not given an explanation of Rome opposing the *"Prince of the host"* which we can now see refers to the crucifixion of the Lord Jesus. He had to wait until Gabriel's second visit, recorded in chapter 9, for the meaning to be made clear. But the message was gently introduced through the emphasis on Daniel's mortality and the need for a sacrifice to bring everlasting life. The passage which follows the vision brings out the fact that Daniel is a mortal man (verses 14-18). An angel spoke to him directly but Daniel still could not understand the vision. It required Gabriel, an angel with the special ability of communicating with mortal men and women, to explain the vision. Another angel, speaking with a *"man's voice"* told Gabriel to enlighten Daniel. Gabriel had the *"appearance of a man"* and addressed Daniel as *"son of man"*.

Daniel went through a symbolic death and resurrection, showing that he was to die before he saw his beloved kingdom. He therefore needed a sacrifice that would enable him to be raised to everlasting life. The wonderful visions of the kingdom that Daniel had received would have no meaning without the sacrifice of the Lord Jesus. He had been told that the kingdom would last for ever, so it is clear that mortal men and women will not be able to inherit it. That is why the daily sacrifices had to be brought to an end. They could never take away sin and death. A greater sacrifice was needed to bring salvation and everlasting life in the kingdom of God.

The desolation of Israel

But in this chapter Gabriel's explanation focuses on the desolation of Israel. What Daniel had to understand was that the transgressions of his nation had not yet reached their fullness. The very sacrifice of his Messiah, about which he was beginning to learn, would be the final act of Jewish rebellion. It would indeed bring salvation, but at the same time it would bring about the desolation of Israel. The ending of the daily sacrifices was important because it would signify the beginning of a long period of desolation in the land. This third prophecy reveals that the final fulfilment of God's purpose would be many years after Daniel's death, although there was never any doubt that God is wholly in control and the end will come.

Conclusion

The crucifixion of the Lord Jesus brought about both the scattering of the Jews and reconciliation to God for those who seek it. The Apostle Paul brings these together and completes the explanation of this vision. Speaking of the Jews he says, *"their fall is riches for the world"* and *"their being cast away is the reconciling of the world"* (Romans 11:12,15). The long period of Israel's desolation, although it appeared hard to Daniel, was actually God's grace in action. It allowed the Gospel to be preached around

The vision	Its fulfilment
The Ram	Medo-Persia: 538-331 BC
The He-goat with large horn	Greece: Alexander the Great 331-323 BC
The He-goat with four horns	Greece: the divided empire 323-63 BC
The He-goat with little horn	Rome and its successors: 63 BC to the kingdom
Broken without human means	The return of the Lord Jesus

the world and for Gentiles to find salvation. But the desolation of Israel grieves the Lord God and will not continue any longer than it needs to, for *"blindness in part has happened to Israel until the fullness of the Gentiles has come in"* (Romans 11:25).

With the New Testament in hand it is easy for us to understand these things but Daniel was utterly confused (verse 27). He fainted and was ill for a time; though he appears to have discussed the vision with his friends no one understood it. He had to wait over ten years until Gabriel came to him again to give the full explanation of the sacrifice of the Lord Jesus introduced in this chapter. That second explanation is what we call the seventy weeks prophecy, and it forms the main part of chapter 9.

The seventy weeks prophecy

DANIEL CHAPTER 9

Daniel prays earnestly for forgiveness for his people. He is given the answer that sins will be taken away by the sacrifice of Messiah. A timetable of seventy weeks will lead to the crucifixion of the Lord Jesus. Again he is told that this will be followed by a desolation of Israel that will last until the kingdom comes.

THE long years passed and there was no further explanation of the vision in chapter 8 which left Daniel so confused. It was not until 538 BC, through the events of chapter 9, that his eyes were opened. Babylon had fallen and the end of the Jewish exile was in sight. In one of the most moving prayers ever recorded Daniel longs for the forgiveness of his people's sins and the restoration of Jerusalem. The answer came immediately but it was not what he expected. It gave an answer to Daniel's prayer for forgiveness and completed the explanation of the vision of chapter 8.

The right perspective is important with this chapter. We shall come to the much-discussed dates of the seventy weeks prophecy later, but the dates are of secondary importance. What really matters is the message that the sacrifice of the Lord Jesus is the only way for human sins to be forgiven. The wonderful visions of the kingdom given to Daniel could only be fulfilled by the sacrifice of his Messiah which would enable men and women to live on the earth for ever.

The chapter is divided into three sections:

- the background to the prayer (verses 1-3)
- the prayer itself (verses 4-19)
- the seventy weeks prophecy (verses 20-27)

The background to the prayer (verses 1-3)

We need first to appreciate what Daniel was thinking when the Medes and Persians took over from Babylon. Well-grounded in the Old Testament prophets, and especially the book of Jeremiah which foretold that the Jews would be in Babylon for seventy years, he knew that period was nearly over (Jeremiah 25:11,12; 29:10). But more than that, the prophets seemed to indicate that when his people returned to their land their sins would be forgiven, a new covenant would be made and they would serve God with true dedication. Above all, the longed-for Messiah would come and the kingdom would be established. (Read for example Jeremiah 32: 36-44, Zephaniah 3:12-15 and Ezekiel 36:24-38.) No wonder Daniel was moved to express the prayer which follows.

Daniel's prayer (verses 4-19)

In a state of fasting, with sackcloth and ashes, Daniel set his face towards Jerusalem. His prayer was selfless, rooted in scripture and devoted to the glory of God. First he confesses the sins of his people and the righteousness of God (verses 4-14).

The opening phrase *"O Lord, great and awesome God"* was from the heart. Daniel must have been very conscious of the power of God. All around him was the evidence that the Lord moves nations to fulfil His word, centred on disciplining His people.

Note that Daniel included himself in his people's sins (verse 5) even though he was among the most righteous of men. The first four verbs in this verse show the progression of these sins from simple disobedience to total rebellion. How well Daniel understood the path the human mind takes once it has begun to move away from God's word!

The problem lay in Israel's unfaithfulness. They had allowed themselves to be drawn away by the attractions of the world around which had brought them *"shame of face"* (verses 7,8).

The solution lay in God's *"mercy and forgiveness"* which doesn't go away, however great the rebellion of man (verse 9).

There were no surprises in what had happened to Israel. The consequences of their disobedience had been set out clearly by the Lord God through Moses at the very beginning (Leviticus 26:14-45 and Deuteronomy 28:15-68). Daniel acknowledges freely that they should have known. God does what He says: *"the LORD has kept the disaster in mind and brought it upon us; for the LORD our God is righteous in all the works which He does"* (verses 10-14).

But then he seeks the Lord's forgiveness (verses 15-19).

There is a fervour and intimacy about this appeal that tells us how closely Daniel walked with his God. His request was presented *"because of Your great mercies"*, showing how much Daniel knew of the grace of God.

But the final basis of his plea to the Almighty is not concern for his own welfare or his people's but for the glory of God. Jerusalem was desolate and it was a city called by God's name. It could not be allowed to continue in that state.

In this prayer Daniel was looking to mediate on behalf of his people to obtain the forgiveness of their sins. But he had to learn, as we all do, that there is only one who can mediate to bring true forgiveness. So the angel Gabriel came again, giving him

Understanding God's word

This chapter gives guidance about understanding God's word (9:20-23):

➤ It follows from prayer and a sincere seeking after truth.

➤ It is a two stage process. We need to know the word of God and then work out what it means. Both of these elements are present here. Daniel was quite familiar with the vision as he had written it down, but he then needed to understand it. The Lord Jesus gives us the same teaching relating to this vision. He says disciples must first read it and then understand it (Matthew 24:15). The meaning will not always be obvious and we must be prepared to do a little work.

the full meaning of the vision of chapter 8 and explaining clearly for the first time in scripture that the whole of God's purpose centres on the sacrifice of Messiah, the Lord Jesus Christ.

The purpose of the seventy weeks prophecy (verses 20-24)

Daniel tells us that Gabriel came to help him *"understand the vision"*, i.e., the vision in chapter 8 where Gabriel came to give him understanding (verse 16) but actually left Daniel completely perplexed (verse 27). The seventy weeks prophecy is therefore an additional explanation of the vision of chapter 8.

Verse 24 explains its purpose: a time period of seventy weeks had been set by the end of which six things would be accomplished. The first group of three was 'negative', being about the need for forgiveness of sins. The second group of three was 'positive' as it was about the introduction of the new covenant. In the first group three separate words were used for sin – all significant as they were included in God's words to Moses when He declared the forgiveness enshrined in His name (Exodus 34:7). They were used again in the commandments for the Day of Atonement (Leviticus 16:21), describing three different aspects of sin and prefiguring the completeness of the forgiveness that was to come in the sacrifice of the Lord Jesus.

1 **To finish the transgression:** the word for 'transgression' means rebellion and describes presumptuous or wilful sin.

2 **To make an end of sins:** the type of disobedience implied in the word for 'sins' is an offence against God but not wilful.

3 **To make reconciliation for iniquity:** the Hebrew word for "iniquity" has the meaning of perversity, a fault.

4 **To bring in everlasting righteousness:** the Law of Moses could never make God's people righteous, never give them everlasting life. By contrast, a person who lives by faith in the Lord Jesus has his sins forgiven and righteousness counted to him which leads to eternal life.

5 **To seal up vision and prophecy:** sealing here is used in the sense of both closing up and authorising. The word is used when Darius used his signet ring to seal the lions' den (6:17). God sealed the new and final covenant through the work of the Lord Jesus which unmistakeably set the divine stamp on his ministry (John 5:36; 14:10,11). Referring to himself as the source of everlasting life, Jesus said, *"God the Father has set His seal on him"* (John 6:27).

6 **To anoint the most holy:** some translations have "most holy place", but this is not in the original text and there is no evidence that the temple was anointed. Prophets, priests and kings were anointed and the Lord Jesus was all of these: he was also Messiah, which means the 'anointed one' (see Acts 10:38).

The seventy weeks prophecy (verses 25-27)

The period is actually "seventy sevens" in the original language but it is normally assumed that seventy weeks is intended. With prophetic time periods it is common to apply the 'day for a year' principle (see page 39). But in each case it is a good idea to test the approach before going any further. Verse 25 tells us that the period begins with a command to rebuild Jerusalem. This occurred at the end of the Jewish exile in Babylon when the Persian kings issued instructions that Jerusalem should be rebuilt. The period ends with Messiah, that is the Lord Jesus. The time between the end of the exile and the coming of the Lord Jesus was a period of approximately 500 years. Seventy weeks (490 days) is 490 years on the day for a year principle. The Jews understood it that way in the time of Jesus and they were much closer to it than we are (Luke 3:15).

It must be said that there are a number of problems in interpreting the seventy weeks prophecy:

- Some key dates cannot be fixed definitely and some are not known at all.
- When does the period start? There were four commandments relating to the rebuilding of Jerusalem after the exile.
- 490 years gives one result for those in the western world who use the solar calendar (365 days in a year) but a

different result if the lunar calendar is followed (354 days in a year). The Jews used the lunar calendar.

Not surprisingly these factors have led to a number of differing interpretations. What is set out here is an explanation of the prophecy which fits the details in Daniel. The seventy weeks is divided into three sections:

Period	The main events
The 70 weeks begins with the command to rebuild Jerusalem, then ...	
7 weeks	the street shall be built again and the wall, even in troublesome times.
62 weeks	No events recorded.
1 week	Messiah shall be cut off. He shall confirm a covenant with many. He shall bring to an end the sacrifice and offering.
... After the 70 weeks there will be an "Abomination of Desolation" until the time of the end.	

The commandment to rebuild Jerusalem

Of the four commandments relating to the rebuilding of Jerusalem after the exile, the one in the seventh year of Artaxerxes in the time of Ezra was in 457 BC. A period of

The 70-year periods of the exile

There are a number of passages which foretold that the Jews would remain under the domination of Babylon for 70 years (see for example 2 Chronicles 36:21 and Jeremiah 25:11). At least two fulfilments of this can be seen, bearing in mind the uncertainty over the exact dates:

➤ Nebuchadnezzar took over Judah from Egypt in 605 BC. Seventy years later Cyrus issued his commandment allowing them to return in 538 or 537 BC. This would have been the one to which Daniel referred (9:2).

➤ The Babylonians desecrated the temple in 587 BC; the rebuilding was completed seventy years later in 516 BC.

490 years from this date takes us to AD 33, which is the end of the "week" when the new covenant in the Lord Jesus was introduced.

7 weeks

The street (or square) and the wall being built again in difficult circumstances relates to the rebuilding of Jerusalem under Ezra and Nehemiah (see Nehemiah 4 and 8:1-3). The rebuilding was made difficult because of the opposition of the Samaritans who tried to hinder the work. We don't know exactly when the construction ended, but it would have lasted approximately the 49 years required by the time period, i.e. to 408 BC.

62 weeks

No events were recorded in the prophecy for this part of the time period. Starting at 408 BC, 62 weeks (434 years) takes us to AD 26. This would have been approximately when the Lord Jesus began his ministry as he was born about 4 BC and started his work when he was 30 years old. It marks the beginning of the final week (7 years) of the time period.

1 week

"He shall confirm a covenant with many for one week". This was the work of the Lord Jesus. The covenant God had made with Israel through the Law of Moses could not give everlasting life. A new covenant had to be introduced (Hebrews 8:7-13). There were approximately seven years between the giving of the Holy Spirit to the Lord Jesus when he commenced his ministry (about AD 26) and to Cornelius' household (AD 33 – the final outpouring of the Holy Spirit). We suggest these two events define the beginning and ending of this final week of the time period.

"Messiah shall be cut off" and *"in the middle of the week he shall bring an end to sacrifice and offering".* Both these refer to the sacrifice of the Lord Jesus when he was crucified by the Romans which was the basis of the new covenant. His sacrifice was perfect and complete so it made the daily sacrifices under the Law of Moses unnecessary (Hebrews 10:1-18).

The Lord Jesus and the "Abomination of Desolation"

One of the references in the seventy weeks prophecy to the destruction of the temple in AD 70 is, *"on the wing of abominations shall be one who makes desolate"* (9:27). The word for "abominations" is clearly used in the Old Testament to apply to idolatry. The use of the word in this prophecy suggests that idol worship would take place on the site of the temple after its destruction by the Romans. Josephus, the Jewish historian who was present in AD 70 tells us that "the Romans brought their standards into the temple area and erecting them opposite the East Gate sacrificed to them there". Forty years before, the Lord Jesus had warned his disciples that this would happen (Matthew 24:15). He urged disciples to flee Jerusalem when they saw these events beginning. This is now history, but the lesson should not be lost on us. Like all the prophets, Daniel's words are there for disciples to read, to understand and then to observe events which are happening around them. It is part of God's support for His people, especially in difficult times, leaving disciples in no doubt that God is in control and His purpose is moving steadily forward.

After the 70 weeks

The Romans continued to rule Judaea after the work of Jesus was complete, but the Jews rebelled in AD 70 and again in AD 132. Rome reacted strongly: Jerusalem was desecrated, the temple destroyed and many towns and villages razed to the ground. All this fulfilled Daniel's vision (8:9-13) and the further explanation of that vision is given by this seventy weeks prophecy. We are told that *"the people of the prince who is to come shall destroy the city and the sanctuary"* and *"on the wing of abominations shall be one who makes desolate"* (9:26,27). The prince was Rome, the "king" of the vision (8:23). This making desolate is the *"abomination of desolation"* referred to by the Lord Jesus (Matthew 24:15 – see page 53).

Finally the prophecy takes us to the time of the end when we read that the desolation will last *"until the decreed end is poured out on the desolator"* (9:27, ESV). The desolator is Rome which means that in some form it must be present at the time of the end, although in this vision we are not given any details. Again we see that judgement on the "desolator" is the work of God, not man and there is a complete consistency with the previous prophecies, as shown in the table alongside.

Conclusion

So Daniel's concerns were addressed. He was reassured that the sins of his people would be forgiven and the everlasting covenant he had read about in the prophets

First prophecy	"A stone was cut out without hands" which shattered the iron	2:34,35, 44,45
Second prophecy	Of the little horn it says, "*they shall take away his dominion, to consume and destroy it for ever*"	7:26
Third prophecy	"*He shall be broken without human means*"	8:25
	"*The decreed end is poured out on the desolator*"	9:27

(Jeremiah 32:40) would indeed be introduced. But he learned that this would not take place upon the Jews' return from Babylon but a long time in the future. And the Messiah he so longed to see as King would first have to go to the cross. The important thing for us is that this prophecy was fulfilled and through its fulfilment our sins can be forgiven. Only because of this wonderful act of grace can we hope for a place in the coming kingdom of God.

Overview of the final vision

WE come now to the last of the four prophecies, a vision which fills the remainder of the book. Although there were no chapter divisions in the original text, the translators have divided it into three chapters, each representing one of the three separate parts of the vision:

- Chapter 10 records Daniel's meeting with the angel who is to give him the prophecy. The angel represents the Lord Jesus and takes Daniel through a symbolic death and resurrection before revealing the message found in the next chapter.
- Chapter 11 is the detailed prophecy itself. It works through the empires of Medo-Persia, Greece and Rome before concluding with the final invasion of Israel by the king of the north.
- Chapter 12 opens with the return of Jesus and the resurrection of believers to the kingdom of God. It is the time of the end and concludes the prophecy. Finally there is an epilogue concerning Daniel himself.

The vision begins and ends with the Lord Jesus and resurrection to life. The prophecy in between is a response to Daniel's prayer that asked about the future of his people and shows that Israel had problems to come. But the overall message is that the ultimate solution to those problems and the nation's eternal future lay in their Messiah as Saviour and King.

The structure of the vision is set out below:

Bible reference	Content
10:1-11:1	Daniel and the angel
11:2	Medo-Persia
11:3-35	Greece
11:36-39	Rome
11:40-45	The northern invader
12:1-3	The time of the end
12:4-13	The epilogue

Daniel and the angel

DANIEL CHAPTER 10

> After a period of prayer and fasting Daniel sees the vision of a man, an angel who is to give him the fourth prophecy. The man is a representation of the Lord Jesus Christ. Having seen the vision, Daniel goes through a symbolic death and resurrection. Only after this is he in a position to hear the words of the prophecy.

DANIEL was in a state of mourning and fasting for three weeks (verses 2,3). We are not told why he was mourning but it may have been because of events back in the land of Israel. It was 536 BC, the third year of Cyrus, King of Persia. Two years earlier the first group of Jews had left Babylon to return to Israel. All had gone well to start with and great rejoicing accompanied the laying of the temple's foundations in Jerusalem. But the enemies of the Jews were quick to sense a danger and *"hired counsellors against them to frustrate their purpose all the days of Cyrus king of Persia"* (Ezra 4:1-5). As a result of this opposition the work was hindered and the news would have saddened Daniel.

The purpose of the vision

Perhaps because of this, or simply because he was still confused by the third prophecy, Daniel was mourning, fasting and praying. Israel's future concerned him and it became the theme of his prayer. We know this because the prophecy was *"to make you understand what will happen to your people in the latter days"* (verses 12-14). But first, there was something from the third prophecy that needed expanding: the work of Messiah in raising the faithful to everlasting life.

The vision of the man

Finding himself on the banks of the Tigris (see illustration alongside, and map on page 59), Daniel looked heavenwards and saw the vision of a man (verses 4-6). It was an awesome sight and clearly a revelation of divine glory. What Daniel made of it we are not told, but we know now it represented the Lord Jesus Christ. The table on page 58 shows a comparison between the man Daniel saw and the vision of the Lord Jesus revealed to John in Revelation. The voice was *"like the voice of a multitude"*, a symbol for the men and women of all ages who are saved in Christ. His body is one but it is made up of all believers (1 Corinthians 12:12). Daniel was about to be shown that he would die before the kingdom came, but as part of the body of the risen Christ he too would rise from the dead and come to everlasting life in the kingdom of God.

The symbolic death and resurrection

So, as in the third prophecy (Daniel 8:18), he went through a symbolic death and resurrection. It was a poignant moment for him, almost ninety years old, conscious of his own mortality and beginning to realise he would die before his beloved kingdom was established. This time the enacted parable was expanded into six parts, divided into two groups of three. The first group was negative, the second positive, a pattern of life out of death we also met in the previous prophecy (9:24).

The first group were three descending stages leading to death, highlighting the helplessness of human mortality:

- Verse 7: as the vision appeared, terror fell on the men who were with Daniel. They fled, leaving him without human help.
- Verse 8: the sight of the man took away all Daniel's natural strength and vitality. He was left in a state of weakness and lethargy.
- Verse 9: the words of the man caused Daniel to fall prostrate to the ground in a deep sleep, symbolic of death.

The second group were three ascending stages leading to life, showing that man cannot save himself from death: it is God's work. Only the angelic intervention brought about Daniel's resurrection to life:

- Verses 10-14: an angel touched him and spoke to him, bringing him gradually to stand upright, although trembling. He listened to the angel telling him that he should have no fear and that he had come to tell Daniel what was to happen to his people in the latter days …
- Verses 15-17: … but Daniel set his face to the ground and became speechless. His lips were touched, enabling him to speak and explain the problem. Daniel felt completely unworthy and was not strong enough to talk with an angel …
- Verses 18,19: … so he was touched and strengthened again. He was urged to have no fear, to be strong and to receive the words the angel had been sent to deliver. With this divine strength and encouragement Daniel was ready to receive the final prophecy.

It was the touch and the words of an angel that brought life out of death, prefiguring the work of the Lord Jesus. From the Gospels we know that the touch of Jesus healed those who were dying (Matthew 8:2,3) and that his words bring life (John 6:63). There is great encouragement for disciples in the work of the angel in this chapter: his words and actions express the spirit of Christ. Read again verses 10-19. See the grace, kindness,

The visions of Daniel and John	
Daniel 10:5,6	**Revelation 1:13-16**
a certain man	one like the Son of Man
clothed in linen	clothed with a garment down to the feet
waist girded gold	girded about the chest with a golden band
	head and hair white like wool, as white as snow
body like beryl	
face like the appearance of lightning	countenance like the sun shining in strength
eyes like torches of fire	eyes like a flame of fire
arms / feet like burnished bronze in colour	feet like fine brass as if refined in a furnace
words like the voice of a multitude	voice as the sound of many waters / in his right hand seven stars / out of his mouth a sharp two-edged sword

gentleness and support for one struggling with his mortal weakness. Truly, this is the mind of the Lord Jesus, *"for we do not have a High Priest who cannot sympathize with our weaknesses … Let us therefore come boldly to the throne of grace, that we may obtain mercy and find grace to help in time of need"* (Hebrews 4:15,16).

What happened through the process of this acted parable of resurrection was that Daniel went from being a mortal man to receiving divine nature (2 Peter 1:4). In symbol he crossed the great divide between humanity and the angels to become part of the divine glory. It must have brought home to Daniel that the impact of his prophecies of

the kingdom was to be deep-rooted indeed. They were not about making this present world a better place, or improving men and women a little, or even about Israel working harder at being obedient to the law. They spoke of a fundamental change. Sin and death have to go: the world will not be at peace until it is ruled by the Lord Jesus and believers who have been given divine nature. Men and women in their natural state will not feature in God's eternal plan, not even through the law. It is only those who, through faith, submit themselves to the healing work of the Lord Jesus Christ and become part of his body that will be raised to everlasting life in the kingdom of God.

Conclusion

This chapter sets the scene for the fourth and final revelation and makes a grand finale to the book. Daniel's prophecies began with the image of a man which looked magnificent but had feet of clay. They end with the vision of a man who is the Lord Jesus Christ in glory, Saviour and eternal King of all the earth. His book began with the kingdom of men ruling over God's people and it finishes with the triumphant ascendancy of the kingdom of God. These were the truths Daniel had been given and, at the end of his long and arduous pilgrimage, he was able to understand (verse 1). Duly strengthened, this elderly man was now ready to receive the longest and most complex of all his prophecies, faithfully recorded for us in the next chapter.

The River Euphrates ran through Babylon and sometimes symbolised the Babylonian Empire (e.g. Jeremiah 13). The River Tigris was at the heart of the Persian Empire.

River Tigris

River Euphrates

Persian empire

Babylon

River Tigris

Jerusalem

A comparison of the northern invaders

Daniel 11	Ezekiel 38 and 39
11:40 – "the king of the south shall attack him"	**38:4** – "turn you round, put hooks into your jaws, and lead you out"; **39:2** – "will turn you around"
11:40 – "the time of the end"	**38:8** – "after many days", "in the latter years"; **38:16** – "in the latter days"; **39:21-29** – the time of the end. Parallels Ezekiel 37:24-28 and Zephaniah 3:8-20, which is the time of the end and Jesus' second coming
11:40 – "king of the north"	**38:6** – "from the far north"; **38:15** – "out of the far north"; **39:2** – "from the far north"
11:40 – "chariots, horsemen"	**38:4** – "army, horses and horsemen"; **38:15** – "riding on horses"
11:40 – "like a whirlwind"	**38:9** – "like a storm"
11:41 – "enter the Glorious Land"	**38:16** – "you will come up against my people Israel"
11:43 – "the Libyans and Ethiopians shall follow at his heels" (or be "in submission", NIV)	**38:5** – "Ethiopia and Libya are with them"; **38:7** – Gog will "be a guard for them"
11:43 – "he shall have power over the treasures of gold and silver"	**38:12** – "to take plunder and to take booty"; **38:13** – "Have you come to take plunder? Have you gathered your army to take booty, to carry away silver and gold, to take away livestock and goods, to take great plunder?"
11:45 – "he shall come to his end, and no one will help him"	**38:18-23** and **39:1-29** – God's judgements on Gog

The detailed prophecy

DANIEL CHAPTER 11

> Following the introduction in chapter 10 we are now given the detailed prophecy. It takes us through the empires of Medo-Persia, Greece and Rome with the focus on Israel. This time there is significant detail for certain periods. The chapter concludes with a passage on the final invasion of Israel from the north at the time of the end.

Alexander the Great

RESPONDING to Daniel's prayer, the angel told him about events concerning Israel from his days to the kingdom of God in relation to the empires we have come to know. Some periods are dealt with in immense detail, others passed over and ignored. No reason is given for this difference although it is probable that the prophecy met the needs of believers in providing support when it was required. The structure of the chapter is:

- verse 2: Medo Persia
- verses 3-35: Greece
- verses 36-39: Rome
- verses 40-45: The northern invader

Our review of the prophecy will follow this structure, although the passage about Greece is quite lengthy and will be broken down into more than one section.

Medo-Persia (verse 2)

The prophecy was given in 536 BC, the third year of Cyrus who reigned until 530 BC. He was followed by three Persian kings:

- Cambyses   530-522
- Gaumata   522-521
- Darius 1   521-486

Then came the fourth, Xerxes 1, almost certainly the Ashasuerus of the book of Esther, who accurately fulfilled his part of the prophecy. He accumulated immense wealth. His father Darius 1 had begun the military campaign against the Greeks, but left it to Xerxes to invade Greece. Xerxes assembled a multi-national army, fulfilling the words *"he shall stir up all"*, and was almost successful in conquering Greece but was finally defeated. There were a further eight Persian kings not mentioned in the prophecy and the empire lasted until 331 BC.

Greece – the beginning (verse 3,4)

These verses refer to Alexander the Great and the four generals who succeeded him. They parallel the equivalent passage in the third prophecy (8:5-8). The additional information given here is that Alexander's kingdom would be broken up, *"but not among his posterity"*. Alexander died young, his brother was mentally ill and his son was not old enough to reign. The empire was initially divided into five but eventually shared among four generals:

1 *Seleucus* ruled the north, including Mesopotamia and Persia.
2 *Ptolemy* ruled the south, including the Levant and Egypt.
3 *Cassander* ruled Macedon.
4 *Lysimachus* ruled Thrace.

Greece: the king of the north and the king of the south (verses 5-20)

Of these four generals, two are detailed in the prophecy since they affected Israel. The successors of Seleucus formed the Seleucid empire with its capital at Antioch in Syria, directly north of Israel and known in Daniel as the "king of the north". The Ptolemies formed their own empire based in Egypt, becoming the "king of the south". There followed one hundred years of rivalry and warfare between these two, from approximately 280 to 175 BC, foretold in great detail in these verses. Israel, of course, was caught in the middle. The accuracy of this prophecy is remarkable and we shall take verses 5 to 9 as an example.

Verse 5: The first king of the south was Ptolemy Soter who abdicated in favour of his son, Ptolemy Philadelphus, a stronger ruler.

Verse 6: The two kings (of north and south) came together in an alliance when Ptolemy Philadelphus' daughter Berenice married the king of the north, Antiochus Theos. To do this Antiochus had to separate from his existing wife Laodice. This put Berenice temporarily in a position of power which she lost when her father died. Antiochus went back to his first wife Laodice. She and her son Seleucus Callinicus murdered Antiochus, Berenice and her son. The Egyptian entourage that went with Berenice to Syria also suffered.

Verses 7-9: Berenice's brother Ptolemy Euergetes successfully invaded Syria to avenge his sister's death, returning to Egypt with a great deal of spoil. The king of the north, now Seleucus Callinicus, launched an invasion of Egypt to recover what he had lost but it failed. He died falling from a horse in 226 BC but Ptolemy Euergetes lived several years longer.

The rest of the verses in this section were similarly fulfilled by subsequent events ending in 175 BC. (For those interested in the details, see *Exposition of Daniel* by John Thomas, pages 48-54.)

Greece: Antiochus Epiphanes (verses 21-35)

The next king of the north has the longest passage in the prophecy. Antiochus Epiphanes (who reigned from 175 to 163 BC) stands out because he intervened directly in Jewish spiritual life. In the end he actively suppressed the Jewish religion, desecrated the temple and persecuted

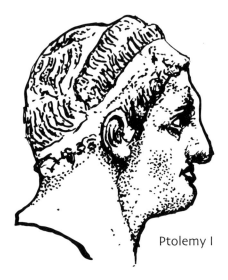

Ptolemy I

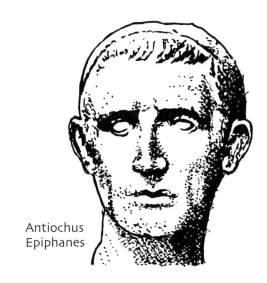

Antiochus Epiphanes

followers of the Law of Moses. Verses 21-28 cover the first part of his reign. He usurped the rightful heir to the throne, so was not given *"the honour of royalty"* (verse 21), then swept south *"with the force of a flood"* and assassinated the Jewish high priest, *"the prince of the covenant"*, who was on a visit to Antioch (verse 22). Antiochus made an agreement with the king of the south, now Ptolemy Philometor, but deceitfully went to Alexandria, part of Ptolemy's lands, and obtained it by intrigue. It was normal for conquerors to disperse the spoil around their generals, but on this occasion Antiochus distributed it among the people to buy their favour (verses 23,24). He then attacked Egypt and Ptolemy was captured. The Alexandrians put his brother Ptolemy Euergetes on the throne (verses 25,26). The two rival kings of the north and south came together but did not achieve agreement because it was not God's will that the conflict should end then: *"it shall not prosper, for the end will still be at the appointed time"*. Antiochus returned north in 169 BC, sacking Jerusalem and stripping the temple of its furniture and gold on the way (verses 27,28).

Verses 29-35 cover the second part of his reign. To understand what happened next we need to recognise that the power of Rome was rising and making its presence felt in the region. Antiochus advanced south in 168 BC and restored Ptolemy Philometor to the throne (verse 29). Philometor promptly made an alliance with his brother Euergetes and they appealed to Rome for help. Rome sent a consul, Popilius, who went to the Aegean island of Delos, boarded a fleet of Macedonian ships and sailed to Alexandria. *Kittim* is the word for Cyprus and can have the meaning of the 'western lands'. Popilius met with Antiochus, reputedly drew a circle round him with his staff and refused to let him out of the circle until he had agreed to withdraw. Humiliated and in a towering rage, Antiochus returned north, passing through the Holy Land and venting his anger on the Jewish people (verse 30):

- His men spent three days slaughtering the Jews. The army destroyed most of Jerusalem, suppressed the daily sacrifice and introduced the cult of Olympian Zeus into the temple which was *"the abomination of desolation"* (verse 31). [Note that this is different from the abomination of desolation in the third prophecy (chapters 8 and 9), which was fulfilled in AD 70.]

- He successfully entered into an alliance with some unfaithful Jews. A few who remained faithful resisted, notably the Maccabees, though many were killed. An edict forbad the Jews from exercising their religion and national customs: circumcision was forbidden, copies of the law destroyed and Jews were ordered to eat swine's flesh. Death was the penalty for disobedience (verses 32,33).

- Initially the resisting Maccabees were defeated but became more successful, eventually winning two significant battles against Antiochus' armies. Many of the faithful refused to give in and were slaughtered for their commitment to the law. This was a test of their faith, an extreme example of the chastening experiences which come to all God's people. It was to *"refine them, purify them, and make them white, until the time of the end"*, that is, the resurrection (verses 34,35).

These events help us understand one of the reasons why prophecy is given: if we can put ourselves in the place of the faithful in those terrible days, we can understand the value and comfort of this history written in advance because it was known to the Lord God. He is wholly in control and His purpose will one day be complete. We can understand the references to the time of the end being at the "appointed time". Their suffering would result in a glorious resurrection to everlasting life in the kingdom of God.

Rome (verses 36-39)

We know that Rome invaded Israel from the northern Seleucid empire, fulfilling the role of king of the north. We identify this king as Rome for two reasons:

1   The king's characteristics match those we have already seen applied to Rome but not to anyone else –

    "speaking pompous words" (Daniel 7:8,11,20);

"pompous words against the Most High … and shall intend to change times and law" (verse 25);

"shall exalt himself in his heart" (8:25);

"shall exalt and magnify himself above every god, shall speak blasphemies against the God of gods" (11:36);

"nor regard any god; for he shall exalt himself above them all" (verse 37);

"the man of sin is revealed, the son of perdition, who opposes and exalts himself above all that is called God or

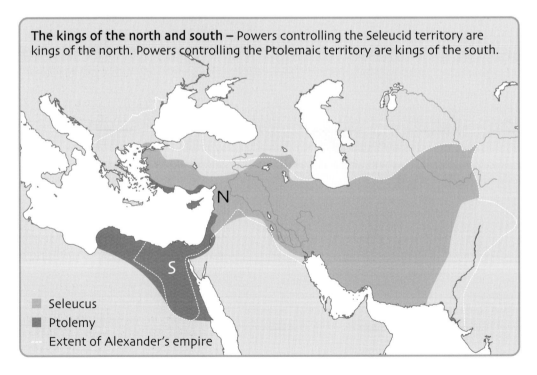

The kings of the north and south – Powers controlling the Seleucid territory are kings of the north. Powers controlling the Ptolemaic territory are kings of the south.

N

S

■ Seleucus
■ Ptolemy
  Extent of Alexander's empire

that is worshipped, so that he sits as God in the temple of God, showing himself that he is God" (2 Thessalonians 2:3,4).

In 2 Thessalonians 2 the Apostle Paul appears to quote Daniel 11 directly and clearly the fulfilment was still in the future for Paul.

2   We are told that this king *"shall prosper"*, which is also specifically applied to Rome (verse 36, cp. 8:12,24).

He will prosper *"till the wrath has been accomplished"* (verse 36). The Hebrew word for *"wrath"* is the same one used for *"indignation"* (8:19). It refers to God's judgement on Israel in AD 70 which led to the desolation of the land for most of 2,000 years. This passage is therefore about Rome between AD 70 and the second coming of the Lord Jesus. Rome in that period in Daniel refers to orthodox Christianity and so we can see how the remainder of the passage applies:

- Verses 37,38: Rome was originally pagan, worshipping many gods. After the Emperor Constantine converted to Christianity the Romans abandoned their idols. This is prophesied in these verses: *"He shall pay no attention to the gods of his fathers"* (ESV) and *"a god which his fathers did not know he shall honour"*.

- Verses 38,39: some characteristics of the new worship are foretold. Though these verses are difficult to translate, the most likely meaning is a reference to the magnificent cathedrals, churches and other buildings of orthodox Christianity.

At the conclusion of the 2,000 years covered by this passage we come to the time of the end, commencing with the role of northern invader.

The northern invader (verses 40-45)

We return to events involving Israel. Daniel is silent on the fate of his land during the 2,000 years of Jewish exile. Jews began to return towards the end of the nineteenth century. What started as a trickle became a flood when the Turks lost control of Palestine in 1917. The British Mandate after the First World War allowed Jews to return, culminating in the establishment of the State of Israel in 1948. There has been conflict ever since but the prophecy we are looking at is specifically about an invasion of Israel from the north. No historical or current events match these verses, so it is a prophecy yet to be fulfilled. First, there is a striking resemblance to another prophecy about the time of the end, the one found in Ezekiel chapters 38 and 39. The table on page 60 lists the details that Daniel and Ezekiel have in common.

- When will the invasion happen? It is specified as the *"time of the end"*. This is confirmed by the beginning of the next chapter which starts, *"At that time"* (that is, the same time as the invasion) and goes on to refer to the second coming of the Lord Jesus and the resurrection.

- Who will be involved? The prophecy follows the pattern of the king of the north and the king of the south but clearly the Seleucids and Ptolemies are long gone! We have seen Rome occupy the position of king of the north so the identification is not restricted to the two original powers. In Ezekiel 38 the invader is described as being from the *"uttermost parts of the north"* (verse 6, ESV). If we look due north from Israel on a map the territory farthest north is in the hands of Russia. This ties in with what we have discovered in Daniel about Rome, since Moscow is known as the "Third Rome" (see "Rome and Russia" alongside). We are told in Daniel that *"he shall enter the countries, overwhelm them, and pass through"* (verse 40) but are not told which countries these are. The invader then goes through Israel, the glorious land. Egypt is his destination, which fits the pattern of the historical kings of the north and south. Indeed, it will be the attack by the king of the south which precipitates the invasion (verse 40). Ezekiel introduces additional powers which we assume will be in support of the king of the south (Ezekiel 38:13). Edom, Moab and Ammon will escape. Today these territories are part of the country of Jordan.
- Why will he invade? We are told that the invader takes *"power over the treasures of gold and silver"* (verse 43), which agrees with Ezekiel (38:12,13).

One thing of particular interest is that he will *"plant the tents of his palace"* within sight of Jerusalem (verse 45). The word used for "palace" is unusual and intriguing. Daniel has selected a Persian word, *apadana*, meaning a royal palace, possibly with religious overtones. Clearly it is more than just a military headquarters and suggests an intention to stay.

Yet *"he shall come to his end, and no one will help him"*, a phrase reminiscent of the fate of the powers representing the kingdom of men at the time of the end in Daniel's first three prophecies. We are not given any details, but the invader's initial successes will be severely undermined by bad news from the north and the east, resulting in his final defeat.

Rome and Russia

Daniel has foretold in four previous chapters (2, 7, 8 and 9) that Rome will be on the world stage at the time of the end. We have seen that this will include corrupt Christianity which will have a significant role. Then, suddenly, a northern power, led probably by Russia appears on the scene. Is there a connection between Rome and Russia? In AD 330 the Emperor Constantine moved from Rome to the east and established Constantinople as his capital. It became the Second Rome, remaining the centre of the Eastern half of the Roman empire and the Eastern Orthodox Church until 1453. In that year it was overrun by the Ottomans and the Christians had to flee. Ivan III, the grand prince of Moscow, married into the family of the last emperor, and decided that he and his descendants would take up the mantle of the Eastern Roman emperor. He adopted the title 'Tsar' which is derived from 'Caesar'. The Russian Orthodox Church was enthusiastic and saw itself taking over the role previously held by the Church in Constantinople. A senior member of the Russian Church sent out a circular in 1492 saying, "God has now chosen grand prince Ivan Vasilevic as the new Constantine for the new Constantinople, Moscow". The continued development of this idea in the years that followed led to Moscow being termed the "Third Rome".

The time periods

There are three time periods in this chapter and none of them is easy to interpret:

➤ 1,260 days (the time, times and half a time in verse 7).

➤ 1,290 days (verse 11)

➤ 1,335 days (verse 12).

One suggestion* is that the 1,260 days is the same as the one we have already met in chapter 7, that is the period of domination by the orthodox church which started with the establishment of the papacy around AD 606 / 607. This period ended about 1867-70. After this Daniel says, *"when the power of the holy people has been completely shattered",* which could refer to the end of the scattering of the Jewish people. The first Zionist conference concerning the establishment of a country for the Jews was held in 1897, which is a period of 1,290 years after AD 606 / 607. The period of 1,335 years has no starting date so we shall have to await events to work out its fulfilment.

*See *The Prophecy of Daniel* by Edmund Green, pages 142-145

The time of the end

DANIEL CHAPTER 12

This is the conclusion of the fourth prophecy. First the vision is completed by telling us about the Lord Jesus' second coming, the resurrection and the kingdom. Then an epilogue brings the prophecy and the book to a close. It also builds a bridge to the final apocalyptic visions in Revelation and confirms beyond doubt that God's purpose with the earth will be brought to its magnificent conclusion.

AND so we are brought to the end, and the setting up of the kingdom of God. The spotlight is on the faithful who have believed the Gospel of the kingdom of God and changed their lives in obedience. They are raised from the dust of the earth to see their mortality fade into history and to take on their eternal role of shining *"like the brightness of the firmament"* and *"like the stars forever and ever".*

The chapter is divided into two parts:

• Verses 1-3: the completing of the vision.

• Verses 4-13: the epilogue to the prophecy and the book.

Completing the vision (verses 1-3)

The phrase *"at that time"* is used twice in the opening verse and is linked to the end of the previous chapter (11:40). The time is defined as when *"your people shall be delivered",* so it is the time of the end and the return of the Lord Jesus. It is the time when Michael the archangel will *"stand up",* but it is not clear in this passage if this is literally Michael working on behalf of the Lord Jesus or a symbol for the Lord himself. Either way, it is the work of the Lord Jesus Christ at his second coming.

Around the time of Jesus' appearance there will be a time of trouble *"such as never was".* Jeremiah has a parallel prophecy. He says, *"It is the time of Jacob's trouble, but he shall be saved out of it"* (Jeremiah 30:3-7). The Lord Jesus quotes Daniel and applies this verse in chapter 12 to the events of AD 70 (Matthew 24:21). But Israel was not delivered out of the troubles of AD 70, so those events were only a foreshadowing of the final fulfilment which remains in the future. Nor do the troubles appear to be restricted to Israel. When the Lord Jesus later refers to the time of the end he includes mankind as a whole (Luke 21:25-27).

Verse 1 (second half) to verse 3 concerns the resurrection, the judgement and the kingdom. The book is a *"book of remembrance"* containing the names of *"those who fear the L*ORD *and who meditate on His name"* (7:10, Malachi 3:16). They will be raised to *"everlasting life"* – the first time this phrase is used in the Old Testament. It confirms what has already been implied in chapters 8-10, that God's people cannot inherit the kingdom in their natural state: their nature takes them to the grave so they must be raised to eternal life. Equally, those who decide in this life to ignore God's will once they have known it will receive *"everlasting contempt"*. The wise are those who *"know their God"* and *"instruct many"* (11:32,33), *"who turn many to righteousness"*, not only through preaching and teaching but through faithful living and Godly example (3:28). In the kingdom of God they will shine *"like the stars forever and ever"*.

The epilogue (verses 4-13)

This concludes both the vision and the book. We return to the angel representing the Lord Jesus; we see him astride the river Tigris, the waters representing all peoples of the earth under the righteous and compassionate government of the kingdom of God. He swears an oath that the end will surely come, an oath with two hands raised instead of the usual one, a mark of divine emphasis.

Daniel is instructed to seal the words and the book. We know why, because, in a similar situation at the end of Revelation John was told, *"Do not seal the words of the prophecy of this book, for the time is at hand"* (22:10). In other words, the events foretold in Revelation were about to start. It follows that events referred to by the angel speaking to Daniel were far enough into the future to warrant keeping them sealed. The mystery is finally revealed when we come to the opening chapters of Revelation. A scroll with seven seals is given to the Lord Jesus (Revelation 5:1-7). The book of Revelation is the record of the Lord opening the seals of Daniel's words one by one and revealing events that were to take place on the world stage. The unsealing is only completed when the kingdom of God is established, so Daniel was told that the words were sealed *"until the time of the end"*.

Then, in a brief final prophecy, Daniel hears that *"many shall run to and fro, and knowledge shall increase"* (verse 4), an example of the remarkably detailed fulfilment of so many of Daniel's prophetic words. How could the final age of this world be better described? It is the age of mass travel and information technology. The world has unwittingly testified to the truth of God's word by describing itself in these last days as a 'knowledge-based society'.

No one was more aware than Daniel of the gulf between human knowledge and the simple facts in the word of God which men and women need to know to obtain eternal life. His share of this word he faithfully set down to be read by all those who are looking for light in a dark world. But his work was now done. He was told: *"Go your way till the end; for you shall rest, and will arise to your inheritance at the end of the days."* It was time for him to sleep in the Lord, in the sure knowledge that an inheritance was prepared for him, to be received from the hand of his beloved Messiah at the end of the Age.

The message of Daniel

The sacrifice of the Lord Jesus

Each of us surely identified with Daniel when he came to understand the need for the sacrifice of his Messiah. No one, not even the most righteous can earn their way to everlasting life in the kingdom of God. The Lord Jesus died for our sins and if we respond to his call through belief of God's word and the waters of baptism then sin loses its power over us. Our faith in this grace and the new life that it brings will lead us to be with Daniel when he is given divine nature and, together with all the faithful, he will arise to his inheritance *"at the end of the days"*.

LOOKING at the state of the world around them people often ask Bible believers why God does not intervene. The message of Daniel is that He will. No one is more aware of the need than the Lord God Himself. The prophet has revealed that God will not allow man's rule to continue for ever but He will set up His kingdom and ensure the earth is ruled as He intended. Man's days are numbered, a time limit has been set and the end is inevitable. The reason for the delay is God's love for man, for He is *"not willing that any should perish"*. Time has been allowed for individuals to come to a realisation of their natural state, turn to the Lord Jesus Christ, change their lives and through him be granted a place in the kingdom. All this we have learned from Daniel as we have taken our journey through his prophecies and the dramatic events that filled his life.

It has been a remarkable journey. The prophet has selected only the facts we need to know because it is important that his message is not lost in the detail. Gradually the panorama of history has acquired shape. Daniel gives meaning to events that would otherwise have been random. He has given us the big picture, the grand scheme, the divine perspective. He has taken us from the morass of detail which is our daily experience and elevated us to the heavens. We have shared his visions, met with angels, looked down on the earth through the eyes of the Lord God Himself until finally the message has become clear.

The Lord God placed man on the earth and set out in His word how He expected it to be governed. Instead, man has chosen to go his own way and the results of human rule are plain to see. Disciples of the Lord Jesus can't wait for it to end. They are uncompromising believers who will settle for nothing but a world at peace, governed by righteousness, justice and compassion. They live for the day when their Master will return, to bring to an end the age of man and establish his Father's kingdom for evermore. The message of Daniel is that they will not be disappointed.

Both the Lord Jesus and the Apostle Paul direct us to the book of Daniel. We have followed their lead in seeking to open the book for disciples today. We have seen Daniel and his friends working out their salvation in the kingdom of men; they have shown us what it means to serve God in a pagan world.

Further reading

THIS Study Guide is intended as an introduction to the book of Daniel. If you would like to learn more, you may wish to try the following books which I have found helpful.

1 *The Prophecy of Daniel* by Edmund Green is a good next step. It works through Daniel following the same exposition as the Study Guide, but gives a broader view of the background history and discusses possible alternative interpretations in some areas of detail.

2 *A Brief Exposition of the Prophecy of Daniel* and Part III of *Elpis Israel* by John Thomas are fascinating and extremely helpful, but really for serious students. There are sections where the prophecy is interpreted in the light of events in the author's time. But the basic interpretation of Daniel has not changed and is set out very directly in these writings.

3 *The Tyndale Old Testament Commentaries – Daniel* by Joyce Baldwin. There is much in this book that provides useful background, particularly concerning the meaning of Hebrew words and information about the empires covered by Daniel.

If this Study Guide has whetted your appetite to learn more about the book of Revelation, there are a number of books that will help you explore its message:

4 *Revelation Study Guide* by Michael Ashton is an introduction to the book of Revelation, explaining the nature of Apocalyptic literature, and the use of signs and symbols to indicate future events.

5 *Interpreting the Book of Revelation* by Alfred Nicholls concentrates on the approach taken to present details of God's unfolding purpose. The author explains the principles that should be followed to interpret the different aspects of the account. Not all of Revelation is covered in this book; as its title suggests, it concentrates only on how to interpret the message. However, in the process, some critical passages are explained in helpful detail.

6 *Notes on the Apocalypse* by C.C. Walker is an extremely useful little work. In a very compressed form it applies the principles set out in the previously mentioned book, and explains each verse. Due to its short length, it does not commit a lot of space to explaining

the method of interpretation that is followed.

7 *Thirteen Lectures on the Apocalypse* by Robert Roberts. As the title suggests, this is basically a transcript of lectures that were first delivered before an audience of interested people. They are therefore very readable, and lead readers through the book section by section, explaining both the message of Revelation and how it can be interpreted.

8 For serious students who want further information about how the book of Revelation expands on earlier scriptures in explaining the unfolding purpose of God, Part III of *Elpis Israel* by John Thomas is a very useful introduction to the author's much longer work, *Eureka* – his detailed and comprehensive treatise on the book of Revelation.

All the above are available from the publishers of this Study Guide.